The Federal Manager's Survival Guide

What You Need To Know About Managing Personnel

Published by
FPMI Communications, Inc.
PO Box 16021
Huntsville, Alabama 35802-6021
(205) 882-3042
Fax (205) 882-1046

ISBN-0-936295-23-6

Cover design by ID Marketing & Design
Huntsville, Alabama

Table of Contents

Chapter Three
Managing Leave & Attendance

Chapter Four
Equal Employment Opportunity

Chapter Five
Managing Unionized Employees

Chapter Six
Using Discipline Effectively

Chapter Seven
Effective Performance Management

Chapter Ten
Safety In The Workplace

Chapter Eleven

Appendices

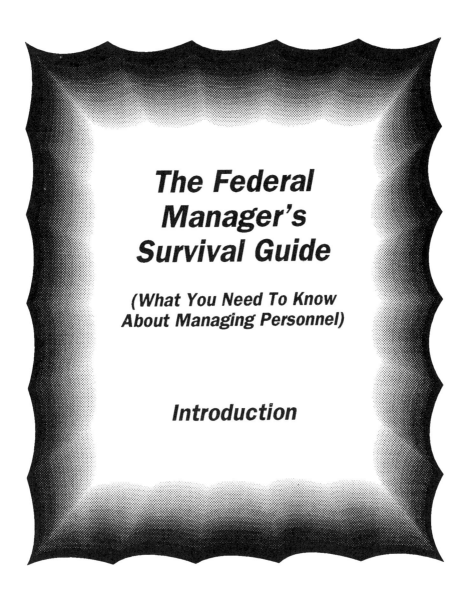

The Federal Manager's Survival Guide

(What You Need To Know About Managing Personnel)

Introduction

Introduction

Overview

If you are reading this, you may be managing employees for the first time in your career. Or, perhaps you never received any supervisory training on the rules and regulations you need to know that will affect all of your employees. This book provides an overview of the rules, procedures and key facts that you will find useful in directing Federal employees.

As you may already know, the Federal government employs different types of workers. These include career civil service personnel, non-appropriated fund workers such as those who staff military clubs and exchanges, and the employees of government contractors, who are not directly employed by the U.S. government. In all probability, however, most of the employees you directly manage will be Federal employees. Accordingly, this book will focus on the civil service, and how to manage employees effectively under the rules governing this workforce.

The purpose of this book is not to make you an expert in personnel management. Rather, it is to make you sufficiently familiar with the basic requirements of leading your employees to enable you to make full use of human resources under your direction in accomplishing your mission.

Management Skills

As a supervisor and as a leader in your organization, you may have already received training in management skills. You may also be familiar with basic leadership principles. These include the ability to motivate, as well as to plan, organize, schedule, assign and evaluate the work of your subordinates. To be successful as a Federal manager, however, you will need a thorough knowledge and understanding of the personnel management system affecting you and those who work for you.

The Civil Service System

The civil service system is an interwoven fabric of laws and regulations that govern all aspects of federal civilian employment from hiring through retirement. To provide a general framework, various statutes—most of which are contained in Title V of the U.S. Code—provide a foundation for the civilian personnel management system. The basic rules governing compensation, hiring, promoting, disciplining and supervising employees are all rooted in this portion of the law.

In addition, various Federal agencies, such as the U.S. Office of Personnel Management, the Equal Employment Opportunity Commission, and others have the authority to publish regulations implementing basic legal requirements. Finally, your agency publishes regulations consistent with the requirements set forth in law and government-wide regulations.

At first, this system appears complex. But you will soon see that the principles underlying the system are quite simple. Your personnel office and legal counsel are available to assist you in finding applicable regulations or providing other guidance in managing employees.

What to Expect

Most of the time you will discover that much of what you can do as a supervisor is nothing more than common sense and good judgment. You can assign work and see that it is done in a timely and efficient manner. You can expect on-time arrival and a full day's work. And you can expect employees to comply with the rules of the workplace. You will have at your disposal ways to reward employees for good ideas and good performance, and the disciplinary tools necessary to correct unacceptable conduct or poor performance.

But there are a number of areas where you will need specific information. For example, employees may choose to be represented by a union. And, if a union represents employees under your supervision, you will have to follow the rules established in a labor agreement negotiated by your agency and the union when making decisions in the course of day-to-day management, such as assigning overtime. Or, if you need to have work done over a weekend or holiday, your agency is likely to have to pay overtime or holiday pay that could significantly impact your budget. Being familiar with these requirements will save misunderstandings and avoid losing time and money to unnecessary workplace conflict.

Managing The Federal Workforce

The Federal Manager's Survival Guide is a starting point. Our goal in this book is to enable you to become familiar with essential requirements necessary to manage Federal employees. **But you should not rely solely on what you find in this book in making personnel management decisions.** Find out who is responsible for personnel functions at your facility. These offices exist to help you accomplish your mission. Each office running these programs keeps regulations governing the Federal workforce and each has a staff of expert personnel specialists who help managers apply the rules correctly. Learn to use them for advice and assistance in making decisions.

Finally, recognize that this book is an overview of the most common subjects you will need to know as a Federal manager. If you would like more information on any of these topics, FPMI Communications has a series of books for Federal managers that treats many of these subjects in more detail.

Chapter One

Classification & Pay

Chapter One

Introduction

Every civil service employee has an occupational classification. This classification establishes the title and primary functions of a job, and sets the appropriate rank and pay grade for it. This system places rank/pay level in the *job*—not in the *person*. Therefore, a Federal employee may move up or down in grade depending on the job (*i.e.*, the position and its classification) he occupies.

It is your responsibility as the manager to determine the appropriate mix of occupational classifications, skills, grade levels, and the numbers of employees in each to accomplish the unit's mission effectively and efficiently. This responsibility is usually referred to as *position management*.

Also, it is the manager's responsibility to ensure that the grade/pay levels established in an organization are consistent with the duties being performed by employees occupying the positions. If the work performed is at a higher or lower level than the job classification, you will want to adjust the duties or work with your personnel office to reclassify the job. In establishing a new position in your unit, or in changing the duties of an existing position, you may be required to write or amend a position description (PD) outlining the primary functions of a position. Personnel specialists then examine such PD's to determine the appropriate classification and grade of the position.

Classification Facts

Civil service law establishes a policy of "equal pay for equal work." This means that jobs of equal difficulty earn the same pay. Classification standards published by the U.S. Office of Personnel Management (OPM) establish benchmarks used in determining the appropriate occupational title and grade/pay level for civil service positions. These standards apply to all Federal career jobs.

The classification system has three broad classification schedules:

General Schedule (GS) for administrative, technical and professional jobs;

Federal Wage System (WG and WS) for blue collar positions;

General Management (GM) for managerial jobs.

There are several facts that will help you understand this system better.

• GS (often referred to as "white collar") positions have 15 levels, GS-1 through GS-15. Each level has 10 pay rates, called steps, in each level.

- Wage Grade (WG) and Wage Supervisor (WS) (often referred to as "blue collar") positions also have 15 levels, but only have five pay-rate steps in each level.

- GM ("general management")positions are only classified at the 13, 14, and 15 levels and have no pay-rate steps. The pay for GM jobs is based on performance ratings within an established salary range.

- For all of these systems, a higher grade level indicates a higher rate of pay, and usually a higher level of authority and responsibility.

Each job has a title, such as accountant, secretary or painter, a schedule (GS, WG, or GM), a numbered series (established by the classification standards) and a grade level. For example:

Accountant GS-510-11
Supervisory Accountant GM-510-14
Painter WG-4102-9
Painter Foreman WS-4102-10
Secretary (Typing) GS-318-5
Secretary (Stenography) GS-318-5

There is a *classification standard* for every major job category and separate standards for supervisory or managerial jobs. In the personnel office that works with your organization, position classification specialists are available to help you make classification decisions in structuring jobs.

How The Process Works

The mission of your organization is reflected in the tasks assigned to its employees. Since a job can have many small tasks, the major duties representing these tasks are written into an employee's position description (PD) by the supervisor and sent to a classifier. The classification specialist finds the standard most closely related to the work and determines the appropriate pay schedule, occupational series, grade level and specific title of the job.

Writing Position Descriptions

Most standards use or will be using the Factor Evaluation System to determine the classification of a job. This system requires that position descriptions include a description of various factors. Once different factors are described, levels are decided and points are assigned. The points for each factor are then totaled and a grade level is assigned to the position. A PD includes a description of the duties in narrative form and a listing of the factors and their weights. The factors are:

> **Factor 1:** Knowledge Required by the Position.
> **Factor 2:** Supervisory Controls.
> **Factor 3:** Guidelines.
> **Factor 4:** Complexity.
> **Factor 5:** Scope and Effect.
> **Factor 6:** Personal Contacts.
> **Factor 7:** Purpose of Contacts.
> **Factor 8:** Physical Demands.
> **Factor 9:** Work Environment.

Each classification standard will apply additional, special factors specific to the job covered by the standard. You should read standards which may apply to the job you are describing before you begin to write a position description. Feel free to ask a position classification specialist for a sample position description or a job standard before setting out to write a position description. (See appendix A for a sample position description.)

Pay careful attention to the classification process, since attracting workers and retaining them is often based on the level and pay-rate of a job.

Position Management

Assigning duties and establishing positions affects the cost of getting a job done. It may also determine your success in recruiting and retaining employees.

In creating a position, a manager should combine similar duties. For example, you do not want to put together a job that requires typing, carpentry and engineering. If you did have such a job, consider the problems it would create. First, finding a person with these varied skills would be difficult. Second, how would you decide the proper pay level for the job? If the pay for a typist, carpenter and engineer were averaged, you would be overpaying for the typing skills and underpaying for those involving engineering.

Effective position management and appropriate organizational structure will help you avoid these problems. As a successful manager, your agency expects you to manage your positions so as to:

☞ Avoid unnecessary layers of supervision.

☞ Assign work at an employee's current grade level.

☞ Create career paths and enhance upward mobility.

☞ Assure that workers are performing useful work.

☞ Use part-time, intermittent, or temporary workers when doing so helps accomplish your mission.

☞ Balance the mix of job skills in an organization (The right mix of supervisors, journeyman, trainees and support personnel to get the job done).

☞ Avoid overlapping jobs and job duties.

☞ Get high quality work done at the lowest cost.

Position classifiers and management analysts are available to help you meet these objectives and develop an effective organizational structure.

Pay

Although you may not have thought about it, Federal supervisors routinely make decisions that affect employees' pay. For example, supervisors regularly make assignments to work overtime, assign employees to different shifts that may involve a shift premium, approve or disapprove payment of environmental pay premiums for exposure to hazardous or difficult working conditions, and assign employees to temporary duties that may carry a temporary promotion and higher pay. Keep in mind that any assignment you make still has to be consistent with the applicable regulations. When in doubt, use your personnel office for assistance before making the assignment.

Overtime

The most common pay decision involves overtime. On an overtime assignment most employees are entitled to 1 1/2 times their normal pay when they work more than an eight hour day or a 40 hour week. In some cases employees earn compensatory time instead of overtime. This means that they get an hour off the job for each hour worked overtime.

Another type of overtime pay involves Sundays or holidays. In certain cases employees may be entitled to double their normal pay rate if assigned to work on these days.

Shift pay

Not all workers have a 9 to 5 job. Many operations require extended hours. One common arrangement is a second shift, usually the first 8 hours after the normal working day, and a third shift, the eight hours preceding the normal work day. Under OPM regulations, workers are paid a percentage of pay to work the second shift and a higher percentage if assigned to the third shift. This type of pay is called a *shift differential*.

Environmental pay

"Blue collar" (wage grade) employees who face on-the-job hazards or extreme conditions, such as intense cold, may be entitled to an *environmental differential*. Sometimes an employee can earn the pay only when the hazard cannot be "practically eliminated." In other cases, employees are automatically entitled to the pay regardless of efforts to mitigate the environmental circumstance.

Other Special Pay Situations

In recent years, OPM has recognized the difficulty of recruiting employees in certain areas and for certain jobs. To fix the problem, special pay rates have been set for some jobs and in some locations. For example, clerical workers in Washington, DC, are paid at a higher rate than in other parts of the country. Engineers and some scientists also qualify for special rates nationwide.

Where To Get Help

To get a briefing on pay rules, particularly overtime, ask your payroll or personnel office. Most agencies have strict controls on overtime and special pay use. Get to know the policies in your organization, and become familiar with the situations in which employees may be entitled to special or premium pay.

Chapter Two

Filling Jobs

Chapter Two

Introduction

When a new position is created or when an existing position becomes vacant, you have several alternatives for filling the job. You can fill the job by advertising for candidates both inside and outside your organization; you may be able to reassign an employee who is already at the same grade into the job; or you may be able to promote an employee from a lower-graded position into the job.

Regardless of how you choose to fill the job, however, you must follow the *merit staffing rules* established in regulations and any applicable labor agreement. Your responsibilities in filling jobs include the following:

☞ Matching the job with the best candidate available;

☞ Insuring that merit principles are observed;

☞ Meeting affirmative action goals;

☞ Developing knowledge of the sources available for recruiting;

☞ Making sound and defensible selections.

The Merit System

Employment in the Federal civil service is based on *merit principles*. Recruiting high quality, qualified candidates and placing them in jobs without regard to their political affiliation is the cornerstone of this system. In most cases, filling jobs through the merit staffing system requires that the vacancy be announced and that candidates be allowed to compete for the job. Applicants from outside the government or those who are seeking a promotion from within must apply, meet specific qualifications requirements and compete for open positions on the basis of their relative qualifications.

The Office of Personnel Management (OPM) publishes qualification standards. These standards are used by staffing specialists in your personnel office or by OPM to screen candidates who meet the basic, or minimum qualifications for a job. When an applicant is rated eligible by comparing her application to one of the standards, she is then referred to the manager making the selection (often called the *"selecting official"*) for consideration.

The Manager's Choices

Federal managers usually have several choices in filling vacancies. These include:

☞ Promoting an internal candidate;

☞ Hiring from outside the government;

☞ Reassigning a current employee at the same grade level who qualifies for your job;

☞ Filling the job on a temporary basis through a detail or temporary promotion of current employees, or the temporary appointment of someone from outside the government;

☞ Transfer of a qualified employee from another part of your agency or other government agency;

☞ Reinstatement of a prior career civil service employee to a job based on prior government employment;

☞ Use of a special system, such as a summer hire or handicapped placement program.

When You Have No Choice

In most situations, managers have full discretion within the rules to select qualified candidates from any appropriate source. There are special situations, however, in which you must specifically consider certain applicants, or even be required to select certain people for a vacancy. These include:

☞ Case settlements or decisions in which a decision is made that an employee has been improperly denied consideration for a job. These cases may involve corrective action to make up for past discrimination.

☞ Placements directly related to a reduction in force in your organization. In some cases, an employee may have a right to a job when she has been displaced.

☞ Employees entitled to priority consideration for a job because they were improperly denied consideration. An example would be a situation where the employee was erroneously found ineligible for a job and therefore was not considered for it.

How The System Works

When a position under your supervision becomes vacant, it is necessary to complete a form (Standard Form - 52) and send it to your servicing personnel office. Most official personnel actions, including promotions, disciplinary actions and awards require use of this form. Before recruiting is initiated, the job will go to a classifier to make sure it is correctly classified.

The form will then go to a *Staffing Specialist*. A staffing specialist is familiar with the job market and will have a feel for the best way to recruit for your vacancy. When you have requested a specific method of filling a job, or if you ask for help, the staffing specialist will advise you of the best source of candidates. If you decide to fill the job within your agency or immediate organization with a promotion action, a vacancy announcement will be published and posted. When the job is to be filled from outside the government, the personnel office will ask OPM for a register (list of candidates). If your personnel office has authority to hire directly from outside, the personnel office will recruit and prepare a register.

Competition

Whenever you fill a job competitively through a merit promotion or from outside the government, the typical way to get out the news is called a *vacancy announcement*.

The vacancy announcement lists job requirements and qualifications as well as any special hours, travel, working conditions, physical requirements and the like.

Outside Hires

If the job is filled by a candidate from outside the government, a staffing specialist from OPM or your own personnel office will determine the eligibility of each applicant and rate and rank them according to a plan set up for this purpose. The names of the applicants are sent to you in rank order. By law, special preference is given to veterans and to spouses of military personnel. Your staffing specialist will advise you of these rules. Often, the staffing specialist will arrange your interviews with applicants.

Merit Promotion

After a job is announced and applications are received, a staffing specialist in the personnel office will determine each applicant's basic eligibility using the applicable qualification standard. This involves deciding whether the candidate has the necessary type of skill described in the standard.

Rating Panels

After eligibility screening of candidates by a staffing specialist, applications are rated according to a *crediting plan* (See appendix B for more information on crediting plans) generally prepared by the manager with the vacancy to fill. The plan is based on a job analysis developed by a staffing specialist. Rating and ranking may also be done by a staffing specialist on a rating panel (or instead of having it done by a rating panel). Rating panel members are chosen for their familiarity with the job. It is common to assign one of the members responsibility for assuring that equal employment opportunity (EEO) requirements are met.

Raters assign points for knowledge, skill and ability based on applicants experience, education, training, performance appraisals, awards, and other job-related factors—as reflected in their applications. In some cases an applicant will be asked to answer specific questions submitted with her application; in others the information will be derived from the application only. Each rater's score for each candidate is kept and compared to the other raters and then these scores are averaged to rank the candidates. Applicants are then placed on a *certificate* in order of their rank.

To limit the number of people under consideration, the certificate will be divided into *qualified* and *best qualified* categories. Usually only the best qualified are referred to the *selecting official*. Sometimes, a recommending or selection panel is used to interview candidates and forward a recommended choice to the selecting official. This more frequently happens with high level jobs.

Selection Considerations

If you have authority to select or to recommend a selection from a list of qualified candidates, you should ensure that written, job-related *selection criteria* are used to determine who will be picked. For example, knowledge of particular computer software, demonstrated ability to complete government travel forms, and experience in operating a particular kind of filing system, might be legitimate selection factors you might specify in selecting an employee for a particular clerical job.

You may recall that the application of a crediting plan determines which applicants will be rated *highly qualified*. Selection criteria are the next step. They represent the manager's specific requirements, and a score sheet for rating the qualifications against the selection criteria of those who are in the final running to get the job. Selection criteria are essential for each job filled, and should be carefully documented.

Selection criteria also put the selection process on a measurable, objective basis, and give the manager data upon which to base a decision. A big advantage of using selection criteria is that the factors provide an outline and starting point for the interview.

If you need to defend a selection, criteria that reflect key job skills, that are measurable or subject to demonstration, and that have been applied uniformly to all candidates are strong evidence that your decision was a proper one. See appendix C for more information on this subject.

Interviewing

The decision to interview may be made for you. The personnel policies in some organizations may require an interview for all promotions, or only those at certain grade levels. In addition, rules may require that if you choose to interview one candidate, you must then interview all. Ask your personnel specialist about the applicable rules on interviewing and selection if you are not certain what you must do.

If you have the option of interviewing candidates, you have a number of factors to consider, including the following:

1. If all candidates are internal, you may not need to interview. If you have sufficient information from applications, performance appraisals and your own observation to make a selection, interviews may be unnecessary.

2. If there are clear distinctions between the front runner and the rest after evaluation of candidates under the crediting plan, you may not need to interview.

3. If there are outside candidates that are unknown to you, interviews make sense.

4. If you want all applicants to feel they have gotten a full opportunity to demonstrate their qualifications, it may be a good idea to interview.

The morale of internal applicants is often a key factor in your decision to interview. When you decide not to interview or only to interview certain applicants, record your reasons for this decision while they are still fresh in your mind.

A Checklist For Conducting Fair Interviews

1. Prepare written questions in advance of the interview.

2. Tie each question to a specific selection factor.

3. If a panel is interviewing, divide the questions among panel members; *do not* let a panelist "ad lib."

4. Do not ask any question that appears culturally or racially motivated or indicates a sex, age or handicap bias. Remember the applicants have read the announcement. If it was accurate, they are aware of the requirements for the job.

5. Avoid questions such as:

• Are you able to communicate with whites/blacks/hispanics?

• Do you plan to have children?

• Is your career tied to your spouse's?

• Do you mind travelling with men, women, blacks, whites etc.?

• Do you intend to retire soon?

• Do you think you can get to work on time considering your .....(handicap)?

6. To the extent practical, ask the same questions of each candidate.

Other Methods Available To Fill Jobs

Reassignment

A current employee at the same grade level who qualifies for your job may be reassigned directly to the position.

Temporary arrangements

If you are filling a job on a temporary basis, you may *detail* (i.e., temporarily assign) a current employee to the position. There are often rules affecting this in regulations and the labor agreement, so ask a personnel specialist what conditions may apply.

You may also temporarily promote current employees for specified periods of time. Again, ask for guidance on the rules.

The government sometimes uses temporary employees. Often a personnel office will maintain lists of these applicants for certain jobs. These appointments are limited to a specified time period or number of hours to be worked. OPM has regulations which allow conversion of these appointments to permanent positions upon meeting certain requirements.

Transfer

Qualified employees from another agency may transfer directly to a vacant position. The process is very simple. Your personnel office is contacted regularly by persons who want to work for the Federal government or who would like to relocate to the area.

Reinstatement

This is another fairly easy way of filling a job. Former employees of the government often have reinstatement eligibility based in their prior government work. They may be reinstated to a position at or below the the grade/pay level they held before leaving government. They must qualify for the specific job and compete if the job would involve a promotion.

Special Programs

There are many special employment programs. Most have their own rules, and generally are easy to use. Summer hire, stay-in-school, cooperative education or handicapped placement programs are just a few of the many options you may want to discuss with your personnel office.

Key Points in Filling Jobs

To the degree you have responsibility for filling jobs, the following are a few steps you can take to keep your placement decisions on the right track.

☞ Be honest and realistic about the requirements of the job.

☞ Be sure the staffing rules are followed.

☞ Make sure the crediting plan and selection criteria are job-related and fair.

☞ Key the interview questions to the selection criteria.

☞ Keep the interview questions on target.

☞ Document the selection/promotion action carefully and completely.

☞ When in doubt, ask your staffing specialist in your servicing personnel office for advice.

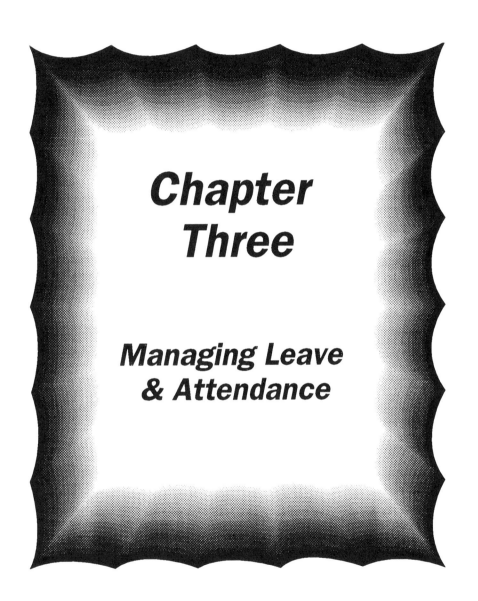

Chapter Three

Managing Leave & Attendance

Chapter Three

Many managers quickly discover that handling attendance and leave issues can become one of their most time consuming functions. The manager's job requires balancing the need to accomplish the work of the organization and accommodating employees who want to get off the job for one reason or another. Federal employees earn annual leave and sick leave, and are sometimes entitled to the use of administrative leave for other allowable functions, such as voting.

Employees tend to view earned leave as a right rather than a privilege, and often assume that it will be okay for them to be away from work whenever any personal matter arises. Although leave is one of the most substantial benefits of federal employment, and it is not surprising that employees want to take advantage of the opportunities it offers, the granting of leave rests in your hands. Annual leave may be granted or denied dependent on the work load of your unit. Similarly, sick leave may be denied unless there is reason to believe an employee is ill, injured or otherwise incapacitated for duty, or has a scheduled appointment with a medical or dental practitioner.

Administering leave has many components as you will see.

For additional information on dealing with leave and attendance issues, see *Managing Leave and Attendance Problems: A Guide for the Federal Supervisor,* available from FPMI Communications, Inc.

Leave administration

In managing leave, your will be required to:

☞ Know the various kinds of leave and the purposes for which each is authorized.

☞ Make determinations on granting or denying leave.

☞ Follow agency guidance and regulation on recording leave usage.

☞ Be accountable for time and attendance records.

☞ Take steps to avoid forfeiture of annual leave by employees at the end of the leave year.

☞ Schedule employee vacations and other leave in such a way as to minimize the effect on the accomplishment of work.

☞ Establish and follow specific procedures for granting leave in your organization.

☞ Conduct counseling sessions with employees who are mis-using or having problems with leave.

☞ Identify and deal with employees who appear to be abusing leave.

☞ Document incidents of leave abuse and follow up with appropriate disciplinary action.

☞ Handle incidents of tardiness properly.

That's a lot of responsibility. To meet it, you will need to become familiar with the basic rules governing leave usage.

Types Of Leave

There are many categories of leave. These include:

☞ Annual leave

☞ Sick leave

☞ Leave without pay

☞ Administrative leave

☞ Court Leave

☞ Jury Duty

☞ Military leave

☞ Voting leave

The types that appear to give managers the most problems, however, are annual leave, sick leave, leave-without-pay, and administrative leave.

Annual leave

Employees earn varying amounts of annual leave per pay period, depending upon their length of government service. They are allowed to store up 30 days in if stationed inside the United States, or 45 days if stationed outside the country. Annual leave of over 30 days is forfeited if not used by the start of a new leave year. This is called the "use or lose" rule. Employees who leave government service receive payment for their accumulated leave in a lump sum upon separation of any kind.

OPM and agency regulations recognize these as proper ways for using annual leave:

☞ An annual vacation for rest and recreation.

☞ Personal and emergency situations such as death in family, religious observance, conferences, conventions or personal business that can only be conducted during the work day.

All agencies have rules that require employees to request annual leave before using it. The determination of whether to grant such a request rests entirely with the employee's supervisor. If workload does not permit or other legitimate factors convince you that it is necessary for the employee to report to work, you may refuse to approve leave. You should only do so, however, where there are genuinely good reasons for turning down the request. The purpose for which an employee wants to use leave is not something you should consider in ruling on a leave request.

Sick Leave

Most employees also earn sick leave during each pay period. But there is no limit on the amount of sick leave that may be accumulated.

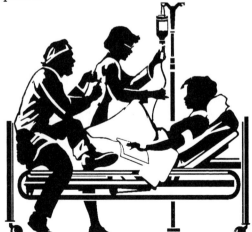

When an employee reaches retirement eligibility, accumulated sick leave may add time to their years of service and increase their retirement annuity.

Sick leave may be used when the employee is incapacitated for duty for medical reasons or when scheduled in advance for medical or dental treatments or examinations.

Agencies rely on supervisors and managers to make a "first impression" determination of whether an employee is genuinely eligible for sick leave. If there is reason to believe that an employee is not genuinely incapacitated for duty, under most agencies' rules supervisors may hold off approving sick leave pending the production of further evidence of illness or injury—for example, a doctor's certificate.

Agencies also have rules that employees are supposed to follow in requesting sick leave. For example, they may be required to call within the first hour of a shift to request sick leave if unable to report for work that day. Although an employee can be disciplined for failure or refusal to follow such rules, you cannot deny sick leave itself merely because an employee breaks the rules for requesting sick leave.

Leave Without Pay

Leave without pay (LWOP) is granted at management's discretion. Employees are not absolutely entitled to use it. In other words, it is up to you to determine whether to grant or deny a request for LWOP.

Employees often request leave without pay when they are have no accumulated annual leave, or do not wish to use their annual or sick leave for some reason. There is no obligation to grant LWOP if doing so would interfere with mission accomplishment. However, if granting LWOP would serve a useful purpose and not interfere with mission accomplishment, you may do so.

Excused Absence/Administrative Leave

Excused absence—or, as it is more commonly known, administrative leave—is most often used in connection with late arrivals or excusal to carry out various non-work functions while still on the clock.

For example, under OPM regulations supervisors may excuse tardiness with no charge to leave when employees are less than one hour late and when their reason is acceptable. Where leave is counted in less than one hour increments (e.g. 15 minutes), supervisors often require use of annual leave for each increment that an employee was late.

Other reasons to excuse absence include bad weather, curtailment of operations or for other special situations, such as recovery from blood donation. The right to grant administrative excusal for non-routine purposes—such as bad weather dismissal—usually is not delegated below upper management levels.

Granting and Denying Leave

Leave is a privilege, not a right. In most instances, you have the right as to decide whether to grant or not grant leave. This is particularly true of sick leave, annual leave and LWOP.

Administration of annual leave and sick leave requires the development of a system. If you supervise unionized employees, remember that it is fairly common for negotiated labor agreements to contain detailed rules for scheduling annual leave and obtaining sick leave. You should be familiar with such rules and apply them consistently.

Dealing With Attendance And Leave Problems

Leave abuse is the single most common basis for disciplinary action. Supervisors have a variety of tools available to deal with these problems. They include:

☞ Counseling employees on tardiness and leave usage, and encouraging them to conserve their leave for times when they will need to use leave.

☞ Requiring employees to schedule leave in advance when the leave is not related to a bona fide emergency or illness.

☞ Writing employees letters of warning when the pattern of leave usage indicates abuse; for example, chronic Monday morning or Friday afternoon sick leave.

☞ Requiring medical documentation to support sick leave requests if a pattern of leave abuse is detected or if a request is made under suspicious circumstances.

☞ Referring apparent leave abusers to the Employee Assistance Program when you suspect the employee has family, financial, medical or substance abuse problems.

☞ Disciplinary action when other options fail to resolve leave abuse problems.

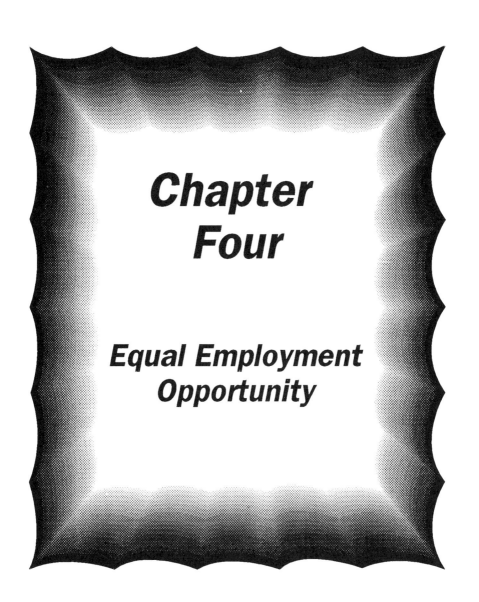

Chapter Four

Equal Employment Opportunity

Chapter Four

Introduction

As a manager of Federal employees you have several major responsibilities for Equal Employment Opportunity (EEO). These include:

☞ Understanding the goals of the Equal Employment Opportunity Program and actively participating in accomplishing these goals;

☞ Creating a work environment free of discrimination;

☞ Developing a positive, problem-solving approach to handling discrimination complaints.

Equal employment opportunity is a program that must be managed. The skills necessary for your day to day success are the same in EEO as in any other management endeavor. When you begin to build EEO efforts in with quality, cost, timeliness and other common performance criteria, you are on your way to running a results oriented, positive EEO program.

For more information, see *The Federal Manager's Guide to EEO*, FPMI Communications, Inc. (1989), Huntsville, AL

Discrimination

Discrimination based on the following factors is prohibited by law in the Federal service:

☞ Race or Color

☞ Religion

☞ National Origin

☞ Age (people over 40)

☞ Sex (including sexual harassment)

☞ Physically or mentally handicapping conditions.

Kinds of Discrimination

There are two general kinds of discrimination recognized by the courts: disparate treatment and disparate impact.

Disparate treatment is the most commonly alleged kind of discrimination. In this type of case, an allegation is made that a person was treated differently from others who were of a different race, color, sex, age, or who were not handicapped. An example of this would be a situation in which an employee charged that he was disciplined more harshly for an offense than other employees of a different sex, age group, or race.

In *disparate impact* situations there is usually a claim that the application of a system (e.g., promotion, training, entrance examination) that appears to treat everyone alike has a disproportionately adverse effect on a particular group. This kind of claim may be made either by an individual or a group. If made on behalf of a group, it is called a *class action complaint*.

An example of a disparate impact allegation is a situation in which members of a particular group contend that their members consistently receive lower scores on a qualifying examination because of language or other cultural biases built into the test.

To defend against an allegation of disparate treatment, the employer must show that it had a legitimate business reason to take the action it did, and that its reason is not just a pretext for discrimination. In the example of a complaint related to a disciplinary action, the employer would either have to establish that the penalty was not inconsistent with those applied in similar cases, or show that legitimate factors justified a stiffer penalty in this instance.

Defending Management Actions

Defending against disparate impact claims is difficult. It often involves statistical studies and complicated validations of the personnel systems the employer is using. In the example given above, the employer will probably have to prove that the test:

☞ Directly measures skills or knowledge needed to do the job;

☞ Accurately predicts future performance success; and

☞ That a test producing less adverse impact would not be effective in identifying qualified candidates.

Affirmative Action

Taking positive steps to increase your organization's employment of minorities, women and the handicapped is a key step in resolving problems caused by discrimination. This effort is aided through the implementation of an *Affirmative Action Plan* (AAP) that establishes program goals and objectives, assigns responsibility for action items, and is used to monitor an agency's success in the effort.

Your role in affirmative action planning will depend on the size and placement of your organization, and your managerial or supervisory level. Whether or not you participate in plan development, your work unit will be affected by the objectives of the affirmative action program. Indeed, your own performance plan may include an element calling for specific efforts to help the agency reach its equal employment goals.

In making decisions to set goals and targets on employment decisions, organizational units look at the percentages of minority, female and handicapped employees at various grade levels and job types. Affirmative action plans are not required to address age or religion, although a court finding of a pattern of discrimination may result in an order requiring that specific actions be taken to correct the problem.

Percentages, by themselves, tell very little about the relative representation of a particular group in the work force. In deciding that a work force does not properly reflect the community's ethnic make-up, factors such as the overall availability of qualified candidates are also considered. For example, the city of Memphis, Tennessee probably will not have as many persons of Asian extraction as San Francisco, California. Consequently, the agency looks at the available work force and assesses whether to identify a particular job as underrepresented in comparison to the available work force. If so, it then targets appropriate jobs for special recruitment efforts to remedy identified imbalances.

Special Programs

Programs directed at improving the employability or opportunity of particular groups are encouraged as a part of an affirmative action program. Specific efforts are reflected by using resources and identifying individuals with a special emphasis program. The Federal Women's Program, Hispanic Employment Program and the Handicap Placement Program are available to help you, and their efforts are usually addressed in affirmative action plans.

Upward Mobility

Upward mobility, another key component of affirmative action, means trying an alternative to traditional promotion systems. Under most upward mobility programs, intermediate positions known as "bridges" are established, and training plans are developed to allow employees who do not directly qualify for a target job to earn through experience and training the qualifications necessary to advance to higher positions.

Handicapped Workers

Disadvantaged and handicapped persons are the subject of a number of special placement authorities. Special handicap appointments with noncompetitive conversion to civil service status after two years of service and the student/summer aide for the economically disadvantaged are two of these programs. See your personnel officer and/or EEO officer to learn of programs available in your organization.

Your Actions

Affirmative action success is often tied to your willingness to take a chance in implementing a program in your organization. You may find that you can obtain additional financial resources or positions if you are willing to hire a handicapped worker or to restructure one of your positions for placement through upward mobility.

Other Actions You Can Take

Commitment to EEO requires action on your part. Here are some ideas that lead to success in EEO:

☞ Make selections based on objective considerations, such as job requirements and the person's qualifications to do the job.

☞ Make day-to-day decisions affecting employees based on job needs, performance requirements and work rules rather than on personal characteristics.

☞ Let everybody know that you are opposed to discrimination and act consistent with that belief.

☞ Treat all employees doing the same job alike. There are obviously differences between people, but the rules should be applied the same way for all.

☞ Keep your personal opinions on non-work issues to yourself. Your opinions on these matters may convince an employee that you are predisposed to favor those who agree and punish those who do not.

☞ Avoid assumptions about groups of people. Saying that you think that all members of a particular group have a particular characteristic—good or bad—guarantees trouble.

☞ Do not tell or condone jokes where the object is a particular group. Judges have frequently found discrimination where there is a history of such activity.

☞ Do not patronize employees. They generally resent a supervisor stating how much he or she understands the problems "you people" have faced.

☞ Being black, white or any other race is a fact not a condition. Do not attempt to use jargon or mannerisms you consider to be part of another cultural group.

☞ Never touch a subordinate or co-worker unless specifically asked to do so by that person.

☞ Avoid sexual gestures, talk, jokes, innuendo, and the like. These can be the basis of a finding that management has permitted the establishment of an offensive work environment—which can constitute sexual harassment.

☞ Never make a management decision based on the sex of a worker unless the situation is governed by regulations.

☞ Deal promptly and decisively with allegations of discriminatory activity or sexual misconduct in the workplace.

☞ Do not allow your subordinates or staff to use or condone any of these practices.

With regard to handicapped employees:

☞ Take positive actions to eliminate barriers in the work place

☞ Do not assume a handicapped person needs certain assistance unless you are expert in the matter. Ask the person what he or she needs, if anything, to get the job done and then try to get it

☞ If a person becomes physically or mentally unable to do the job, get immediate advice from specialists in the area on how to handle the problem.

☞ If you have reason to believe that an employee's performance is affected by alcohol or other substance abuse problems, refer him or her to the Employee Assistance Program and seek assistance from your personnel staff on how to otherwise deal with the problem. Alcohol and drug abuse are handicapping conditions under the law. Employees having these conditions are protected from discrimination and entitled to reasonable accommodation.

Discrimination Complaints

No matter how well you perform in meeting equal opportunity goals or in advancing anti-discrimination policies, an employee under your direction or an applicant for a job you are filling may perceive a decision you have made as discriminatory and file an EEO complaint. Let's look at the complaint process and how you can deal with a complaint in a professional and positive manner.

Your goal in dealing with a discrimination complaint will be to reach a resolution that is equitable to the complainant, acceptable to you, and perceived by the rest of the workforce as a fair and proper outcome.

Get Your Thoughts Together

As soon as you have the suspicion that one of your decisions may be challenged, do the following before you talk about it with anyone:

1. Review the decision you made and the actions leading up to it.

2. Gather any documents that relate to the matter including notes or memos for record you may have written.

3. Make a list of the people involved, their roles and knowledge of the action.

4. Compose your thoughts on the challenged decision and write down the reasons you made the decision and what factors influenced it.

5. Do not try to "be a lawyer." Simply address each of these steps in a series of statements written in a style you normally use in your written communications.

Understand How the Process Works

Discrimination complaints go through various stages in processing. The law provides for administrative handling before the complainant is permitted to challenge an action in the courts. Administrative handling is the way your agency and the Equal Employment Opportunity Commission deal with an allegation.

Counseling

Before an allegation can be formally made to an outside agency, the individual making the allegation must contact an EEO counselor. This is designed to permit an attempt at an informal resolution to their problem. Most complaints are resolved at this stage in the process.

It is the job of an EEO counselor to seek a resolution. A counselor does not represent a complaining employee or serve as an investigator or prosecutor. The EEO counselor is trained to find out what is troubling the employee making the allegation, and to seek a resolution to the problem.

Meeting With The EEO Counselor

If an EEO counselor requests a meeting, you should prepare carefully. Ask the counselor what will be discussed, and what information will be needed at the meeting.

If you have been identified in a complaint as the management official responsible for the alleged discriminatory act, you are entitled to know—and should ask about—the following:

1. The basis of the allegation (e.g., race, color, religion, or sex).

2. The specific action or decision that has been alleged to be discriminatory.

3. The specific facts that support the allegation; that is, what made the person think he or she was the subject of discrimination?

4. The specific remedial action(s) that would result in settlement and withdrawal of the allegation.

If counseling is unsuccessful the employee may file a formal complaint. Once the matter becomes a formal complaint, it is wise to seek the advice of your personnel office or legal counsel whenever you are contacted about the matter. Discrimination cases often involve lengthy investigations, and may come to a hearing quite some time after the fact. Consequently, you should document any facts that will be important to recall at a later date. Finally, bear in mind you are entitled to a personal representative at any stage in the process.

Also, if you are planning to settle the allegation informally, you should seek the advice of your agency representative. This will ensure any action you may choose to take is legal and will not create additional problems for your or your organization.

Chapter Five

Managing Unionized Employees

Chapter Five

Introduction

One of the more difficult adjustments managers must make is learning how best to deal with unions and union-represented employees in the workplace. This chapter provides an overview of the key points you need to understand if any of the employees under your direction are represented by a union.

Basic Concepts

The majority of non-supervisory employees in the Federal service are eligible to be represented by a union. This entitlement is based on Chapter 71 of Title 5 U.S. Code, which is known as the Federal Labor-Management Relations Statute. We will refer to it simply as the law or **Statute** from this point on.

The law establishes a tripod of rights: Employee rights, union rights, and management rights. The following is a brief explanation of them.

For more information, see *The Supervisor's Guide to Federal Labor Relations*, FPMI Communications, Inc., Huntsville, AL

Employee Rights

The statute provides that eligible employees may choose to group themselves together and to determine, through closed ballot election, whether to have a particular union represent them. If they choose to do so, the particular group—regardless of whether it consists of the employees of a particular shop, a set of occupations, or all eligible employees in an agency or installation—is called a **bargaining unit**. The particular **union** selected to represent the group is then designated as the **exclusive representative** of all employees in the bargaining unit, regardless of whether they vote for, join or support the union.

The law also guarantees employees the right to decide whether to join the union, and whether to assist it by serving as a union representative. Most important, the law provides that employees may exercise these rights **free of any influence, coercion or reprisal by management officials**. In short, in the Federal service managers are prohibited from attempting to influence the employees' choice in such matters, either by word or deeds. Consequently, **statements** to employees that could reasonably be expected to discourage them from exercising union-related rights, or **actions**—such as discipline, non-selection for promotion, or lowered performance ratings—that are based on an employee's union activity, are ruled out by the law.

Union Rights

Right to Bargain

When a group of employees has chosen to be represented by a union, the selected union automatically gains certain rights under the law. The most important of them is the **right to bargain** with agency management concerning the **conditions of employment** of the represented employees. What this means is that the union can require management to negotiate on a broad range of issues involving the **personnel rules** that apply to employees (such as rules concerning promotion, leave use, or discipline), as well as various **working conditions** that are part of the work environment (for example, heat, air conditioning, safety equipment, smoking rules, parking arrangements). The agency is legally bound to bargain in good faith with the union on all matters that are legally negotiable, but it is not obligated to agree to any particular proposal if it feels it would be unwise to do so.

Right to Represent Employees

In addition to the right to bargain, under the law the union is also granted **the right to represent employees** in a variety of dealings with management officials. This includes the investigation and presentation of grievances; assistance during investigative meetings that could lead to discipline; and service on various labor-management committees—for example, a safety and health task force.

Management Rights

The third component of rights established by the Statute is that of **management rights**. In effect, the law extends to employees the right to organize, and to unions the right to represent employees through bargaining. But it also specifies that agency management is responsible for the effective and efficient operation of the agency and the accomplishment of its mission. To help agencies achieve that objective, the law provides managers with an extensive list of management rights.

The management rights outlined in the Statute can be grouped into three primary areas: Mission/ organizational rights; work assignment rights; and personnel management rights.

Mission/Organizational Rights

Under these rights agency managers are granted the authority to determine the mission of the agency and its components; to decide how to organize people, dollars and equipment most effectively; to determine what tools, technology and work methods should be used; to establish the numbers, types and grade levels of employees that should be employed in various parts of the organization; and to determine the internal security measures that should be adopted to protect employees and property.

Work Assignment Rights

Federal managers are also granted extensive control over the assignment of work. It is your right to determine what work will be accomplished, when and where it will be done, which personnel will be assigned to various parts of the organization, what duties will be assigned to particular positions or occupations, and the qualifications that will be required to perform various duties or assignments.

Personnel Management Rights

Finally, management officials are provided statutory authority to make and carry out a broad range of personnel management decisions. Included, for example, is the right to determine whether to fill a position, or to promote, discipline, reward, detail or layoff employees for lack of work.

In short, the Federal labor relations law provides managers virtually every management tool necessary to meet mission requirements effectively and efficiently.

Note, however, that although managers possess the authority to make decisions necessary to accomplish the mission, it must be exercised consistent with negotiated rules governing its use. For example, you have the right to decide whether to fill a vacant position, but may have to follow specific negotiated procedures—often contained in a labor agreement—in advertising and filling the job. Similarly, a working condition—such as a negotiated rest period or a parking arrangement—generally must be observed as bargained.

Key Labor-Management Relations Situations

Managers generally become involved in labor-management relations in the following four situations:

☞ Changes in the workplace

☞ Meetings with represented employees

☞ Decisions involving the labor agreement

☞ Grievances and complaints.

Each situation will be discussed briefly below.

Changes in the Workplace

Management is constantly involved in the introduction of change into the workplace. The number of people may be increased or decreased; operations are reorganized and duties shifted; new tools, technology and work procedures are adopted; shifts are added and dropped; and various personnel rules, such as those governing smoking, are changed or introduced.

Most, though not all, such changes fall within the realm of management's statutory rights. Nevertheless, under the law the union has the right to bargain with management on ways to deal with the *impact* upon employees when management makes a change that will alter personnel rules or working conditions. Failure to understand this point accounts for the overwhelming majority of unfair labor practice disputes throughout the Federal service every year.

This means operating managers must keep in mind two things when contemplating changes in a unionized organization. First, that it is necessary to determine whether an intended change will alter represented employees' working conditions or change a personnel rule that applies to them. Second, if it appears likely or possible that it will do so, it is important to **notify the union of the intended change *before* it is put into effect**. If the union responds to the notification by requesting to negotiate, the agency is legally obligated to meet and to make a sincere effort to reach agreement on all negotiable proposals that are presented.

Your agency's Personnel Office and/or the Labor/ Employee Relations Office can provide additional information and assistance in dealing with such situations.

Meetings With Represented Employees

The bulk of face-to-face communications with employees generally involves routine work-related matters; for example, work assignments and instructions, performance feedback and suggestions, and the updating of job-related information. The law provides for no union involvement in a supervisor's direct communications with employees on such routine matters.

But the Statute does specify two particular situations involving direct communication with employees in which a union has the right to be present and to take an active part. They are known as **formal discussions**, and **investigatory**—or **Weingarten**—meetings.

Formal Discussions

The idea behind formal discussions is simple. Basically this provision is designed to ensure that management officials will deal directly with the employees' elected union representatives on all bargainable matters, and will not leave the union out of significant discussions with employees on matters that fall within the union's area of representational responsibility.

Accordingly, in meetings with bargaining unit employees that meet *all three* of the criteria outlined below, managers are obligated to inform the union in advance of the meeting and to allow it to have a representative attend and actively participate. The three key criteria are:

1. **Attendance**. Both a management representative—such as a supervisor, manager, personnel specialist—and one or more bargaining unit employees will be involved in the meeting.

2. **Topic**. The matters to be discussed will include either the personnel rules and/or working conditions of represented employees, or a grievance or appeal that has been filed by a bargaining unit employee.

3. **Formality**. The meeting will be formal in nature; that is, not a casual, unplanned conversation, but rather a serious, organized discussion of conditions of employment or a grievance/appeal. In gauging whether a meeting is "formal," the Federal Labor Relations Authority (FLRA) looks at such matters as whether the meeting was scheduled in advance, whether there was an established agenda, how many persons attended the meeting, whether attendance was mandatory, and whether formal notes or minutes were taken.

Relatively few meetings between managers and employees meet all three criteria. Those that do, however, require advance notification to the union.

Investigatory (Weingarten) Meetings

The second special communication situation involves discussions with bargaining unit employees that are *investigatory* in nature, and could reasonably be expected to lead to discipline. The law establishes four criteria by which such situations may be recognized.

1. **Attendance**. Both a management representative (manager, supervisor, personnelist, investigator) and a bargaining unit employee are present.

2. **Nature of Discussion**. Investigatory, in that questions are being asked in an effort to ascertain facts.

3. **Reasonable Fear**. Based on the totality of circumstances *the employee* could reasonably fear that discipline might be forthcoming, perhaps dependent upon his/her answers.

4. **Request for Representation**. The employee makes a request for, or at least some mention of, union representation.

If all four of these criteria are met you must allow the employee to have a union representative present before you continue asking questions.

When faced with either a formal discussion or Weingarten meeting situation, do not hesitate to contact the Personnel Office and/or Labor/Employee Relations Office for advice and assistance.

Decisions Involving the Labor Agreement

Managers are not always aware that day-to-day decisions affecting employees may involve the application of rules established in the labor agreement—or, as it is often known, the union contract. For example, decisions as to which employees to pick for an overtime assignment, how to resolve a leave-scheduling problem, or when to authorize pay at a higher rate for an employee detailed into a higher level job, all are likely to be governed by provisions contained in the labor agreement.

The manager has three roles: To know the contract; to interpret and apply its provisions correctly; and to enforce these provisions as management intended. The key question is *how* to go about interpreting and applying the contract in a correct, consistent manner. The following steps outline an approach favored by labor relations professionals and arbitrators who rule on contract disputes.

Step 1: Find the rule. If a situation—such as one of those mentioned above—calls for a decision and you are not certain of the correct answer, look first into the labor agreement to see if any of its provisions seem to cover the situation. For example, to deal with a leave scheduling dispute, check for provisions on Annual Leave.

Step 2: Determine Clarity. Determine whether a provision or rule found in the contract is absolutely clear, or whether it is vague enough to allow for more than one meaning. If there is no rule in the contract, or if contract language is vague enough to allow for more than one interpretation, it may be necessary to obtain additional information.

Step 3: Check Further. If a contract provision is unclear, before making a decision it is always advisable to check whether such situations have come up before and how they were handled. It may be that there is an established pattern amounting to an unwritten rule (usually known as a *past practice*). Or there may have been a previous grievance or arbitration decision interpreting the rule. If so, it is usually best to follow the established path.

Step 4: Obtaining Advice/Assistance. If a clear meaning of the rule is not apparent, the Personnel and/or Labor/Employee Relations Office can be helpful in advising you on how to proceed.

Grievances and Complaints

The final situation which brings managers into contact with labor-management relations is that of dealing with grievances and complaints. Generally speaking, such disputes arise in one of two formats: A grievance filed under the labor agreement's grievance procedure, or an unfair labor practice charge (ULP) filed with the Federal Labor Relations Authority (FLRA). The formats are quite different. But you may become involved and play a key role in dealing with both types of disputes. Each is briefly described below.

Grievances

Every Federal sector labor agreement contains a grievance procedure that permits employees and the union to raise contentions that a contract provision, associated past practice, or a law or regulation has been improperly interpreted or applied.

Most grievance procedures consist of a three or four step process that allows the grievant and/or union to present an issue to managers at several levels in an effort at obtaining a resolution. In most cases, grievances must first be filed with the immediate supervisor. Only if the matter is not satisfactorily worked out at that level may the grievant/union elevate the issue to the succeeding levels.

If the grievant or union does not obtain what it views as a satisfactory resolution in the grievance process, contracts allow the union to request the matter be presented to a neutral *arbitrator*—sort of a rent-a-judge—for a final, binding decision.

Clearly, the primary function of the grievance procedure is to provide an orderly and acceptable mechanism for challenging management decisions under the labor agreement. From the union point of view, the grievance and arbitration machinery exist primarily as the means of enforcing the terms of the labor agreement. From the management point of view, they exist to channel conflict into an acceptable and orderly framework for resolution.

ULP Procedure

The ULP process is the mechanism for enforcing rights provided under the Federal Labor-Management Relations Statute. For example, if a party refuses to bargain as required, or engages in discriminatory actions based on an employee's union activity, a ULP charge can be filed since such actions would violate the requirements of the Statute.

Unlike the grievance process, the ULP procedure brings an outside agency—the FLRA—into the situation immediately. Following the filing of a charge an FLRA agent contacts the agency and commences an investigation. Depending on the findings of the investigation, the matter may then be scheduled for a formal hearing before an administrative law judge. If the agency is ultimately found in violation of the law, any of several remedial actions may be ordered, including the reversal of a management action or the reinstatement of employees with backpay and interest.

Dealing With Union Officials

Involvement in day-to-day contract application issues and grievance handling usually brings managers face-to-face with union officials. Most officials will be agency employees who spend part of their time serving as union representatives. In dealing with such officials it is important to bear in mind two important points.

First, while officially representing the union or employees, union representatives are operating more as an equal of their management counterparts than as subordinates. Consequently, they are entitled to more latitude than might be acceptable in routine superior-subordinate dealings. For example, a steward is within the bounds of protected activity while presenting a grievance if he told you that he felt your decision was stupid and incorrect. While such phrasing would probably be unacceptable behavior in a regular workplace situation, within the context of a grievance meeting it is usually allowed.

The second point to bear in mind is that your agency's labor agreement probably spells out specific rules that apply to the request and granting of on-the-clock time—generally referred to as *official time*. It is important to understand and apply these rules fairly and consistently. Failure to do so can lead to a loss of control over the use of worktime for representational activities.

For more information on how to deal effectively with union officials contact your Personnel and/or Labor/Employee relations office.

Chapter Six

Using Discipline Effectively

Chapter Six

Introduction

To maintain the effectiveness and morale of any workforce, you may find it will be necessary to take disciplinary action. Federal employees have recourse to a number of grievance and appeal mechanisms available to them and when you take an action, you are likely to find yourself involved in one or more appeal processes.

Contrary to popular mythology, it *is* possible to use discipline to correct unacceptable behavior of a civil service employee. But in order to use this tool effectively, it is necessary first to understand several basic concepts.

This chapter will introduce the basic principles you need to apply in order to use discipline appropriately and effectively. Before initiating disciplinary action, however, we *strongly* recommend that you obtain advice and assistance from your personnel office.

For more information on taking disciplinary action, see *The Federal Manager's Guide to Discipline*, FPMI Communications, Inc (1991), Huntsville, AL

Corrective Action

A fundamental principle underlying the use of discipline is that disciplinary penalties are employed *to correct inappropriate or unacceptable behavior, not to punish the employee* for her transgressions. This principle is important to understand because outside authorities who often review challenges to disciplinary action—such as the courts, labor arbitrators, and other third parties—use it to determine whether discipline was necessary, and if so, whether the penalty was reasonable.

Progressive Discipline

Closely related to the principle of corrective action is the notion that, in the overwhelming majority of instances, disciplinary penalties should *progress* in severity. The idea, again, is a simple one: Since disciplinary action is undertaken to correct inappropriate behavior, managers should apply the minimum penalty likely to bring about the desired change.

If the behavior occurs again, progressively stiffer penalties should be used in an effort to produce the desired correction. Severe penalties for first offenses—such as removal from the Federal service—generally withstand review only in the most severe situations.

Taken together, the principles of *corrective* and *progressive* discipline rule out using excessively harsh or arbitrary penalties. Consequently, it is necessary to weigh numerous factors in deciding whether to impose disciplinary action to correct a problem.

Performance vs. Conduct

Federal regulations distinguish *performance* and *conduct* problems. *Performance* problems involve situations in which an employee is not performing his duties at an acceptable level of quantity, quality or timeliness. In these cases the employee may or may not be able to perform up to expectations.

In *conduct* situations, an employee may be performing her work fully up to job expectations, but breaking established rules. For example, coming to work late or leaving early, refusing to follow orders, or leaving the work site without permission. In such cases the employee may be fully capable of performing well, but nonetheless breaks workplace rules.

The distinction is important in that misconduct (rule-breaking) is dealt with through disciplinary action, while performance problems (failure to meet quantity, quality, timeliness expectations) are dealt with differently. Disciplinary actions, such as reprimands and suspensions without pay, are used to correct misconduct; performance improvement coaching, training, and counseling are used to improve performance deficiencies. Your personnel office can assist you in deciding how to respond.

Deciding Whether To Discipline

The first decision to make in deciding whether to discipline an employee is whether the unacceptable behavior is misconduct or poor performance. In most, cases, that is simple. And, in most situations, misconduct is involved rather than poor performance.

If the situation involves apparent misconduct, the next question to ask is whether *any* discipline is appropriate; that is, whether any level of disciplinary action may be supported by sufficient facts to pass muster as justifiable discipline before an outside party.

The key factors such parties consider in determining whether an employee was justly disciplined include the following:

1. *Do the facts establish that the employee did—or failed to do—the things claimed by the agency?* If not, discipline cannot stand, since the employee is presumed innocent unless proven "guilty."

2. *Did the employee's behavior, if proven, violate an established rule, regulation, or requirement?* If not, any disciplinary action is doomed to reversal on review.

3. *Did the employee know—or should he have known—of the rule, regulation or requirement?* If the rules have not been adequately communicated to employees, they cannot be held accountable for compliance with them.

4. *Has the rule been enforced consistently?* If not, discipline against an employee is likely to be considered arbitrary or discriminatory by a third party, regardless of how well the case is proven.

Only if a potential disciplinary action can meet *all* of the requirements outlined above should you consider the appropriate penalty. If you cannot answer "yes" to any of these questions, *any* disciplinary penalty is likely to be overturned if challenged through a grievance or appeal.

Selecting An Appropriate Penalty

Several factors come into play in determining an appropriate penalty. Included among them are the basic concepts of corrective, progressive discipline. That is, penalties must be selected with an eye to applying the minimum discipline likely to be necessary to correct the offense.

Second, you must also consider fairness and consistency. In short, penalties should be reasonably consistent with the discipline effected in similar situations against employees with similar records.

This means that you must carefully weigh a number of things in determining how severe a disciplinary penalty should be, including:

☞ Nature and severity of the offense;

☞ Employee's previous record;

☞ Employee's potential for rehabilitation;

☞ Penalties imposed on other employees in similar situations;

☞ Agency penalty guidelines.

Again, your personnel office can be very helpful in identifying a range of appropriate penalties for the particular situation you are facing.

Procedural Issues

Federal personnel regulations, and some labor agreements require that following specific procedures in investigating, recommending and carrying out disciplinary action. The following is a brief outline of procedures to bear in mind.

In all but the most minor infractions, you must conduct a reasonably complete investigation of the facts of the case before recommending or deciding upon discipline. If the facts developed through an investigation indicate disciplinary action may be necessary, it then becomes appropriate to recommend a particular disciplinary penalty.

In most situations that may involve formal discipline that is more severe than a written reprimand (for example, a suspension from duty, downgrade or removal), one level of management recommends a disciplinary penalty (the *recommending official*) and a higher level manager makes the final decision (the *deciding official*). Following a formal, written proposal to discipline an employee, she is entitled to provide a written and/or an oral response before the deciding official makes a final decision. The final decision may endorse the original recommendation, reduce the recommended penalty, or decline to impose discipline at all.

Following the imposition of disciplinary action, the employee may challenge the decision through a variety of mechanisms, including the agency or labor agreement grievance procedures, the Merit Systems Protection Board (MSPB) appeal procedure, or through the Equal Employment Opportunity Commission (EEOC) appeal process. Generally, employees are entitled to use only one procedure to appeal a particular action.

Employees Represented By A Union

Several additional factors come into play in dealing with employees represented by a union.

First, during the investigation of possible misconduct a bargaining unit employee is entitled to the assistance of a union representative when being questioned if he could reasonably fear discipline and asks to have a representative present. This is often referred to as the *"Weingarten"* right.

Second, the labor agreement covering a particular group of employees may establish different or additional procedural requirements that must be followed in the disciplinary process. For example, the contract might grant employees the right to a personal meeting with the Deciding Official before a final decision is made, or it may allow a temporary stay of discipline pending appeal.

Third, labor agreements usually allow either a disciplined employee or the union to grieve a disciplinary action, and, if the matter is not satisfactorily resolved, to place the issue before a neutral, outside arbitrator who is empowered to render a final, binding decision on the matter.

See Chapter Five on Managing Unionized Employees for additional information.

Common Problems

As might be expected, employees challenge most disciplinary actions, contending either that discipline was not warranted, or that the penalty imposed was too harsh, or that proper procedures were not followed—or some combination of all three assertions. Although the majority of disciplinary actions withstand such challenges, a surprising percentage are modified or reversed. Generally such modifications and reversals stem from one or more of the following common mistakes.

1. *Failing to assemble sufficient evidence that the employee is culpable of the charged offense.* Suspicion or "gut level knowledge" of guilt is not enough.

Moral: Be sure you can back up suspected rule violations with convincing facts that can be presented to an outside judge, if necessary.

2. *Inconsistently applying the rules.* Regardless of whether you can prove an employee's actions in violation of a rule—such as late arrival for work—discipline usually will not stand if the employee can show that others have been permitted to break the rule without similar disciplinary action.

Moral: Enforce rules evenhandedly; if the enforcement of a rule has slipped, announce your intention to enforce it *before* imposing discipline against employees.

3. *Prematurely announcing disciplinary intentions.* Sometimes managers have made the mistake of flatly telling an employee "on the spot" that he will be disciplined or fired; *i.e.*, *before* an investigation and appropriate recommendations have been completed. Some labor arbitrators have viewed such statements as evidence that subsequent discipline was not based on a full and fair consideration of the facts, and have reversed on that basis alone.

Moral: Avoid outright predictions, promises or threats of specific penalties.

4. *Failing to follow procedural requirements.* Disciplinary actions are routinely reversed where procedural errors in the handling of the action produce "harmful error." Common examples of such errors include failure to allow union representation as required, or taking too long to carry out discipline following an investigation.

Moral: Check procedural requirements in regulations and the labor agreement *before* acting; work closely with your personnel specialists to make sure the bases are fully covered.

5. *Inadequately explaining the penalty determination.* In response to any grievance or other appeal of a disciplinary action, managers are required to explain not only *why* discipline was deemed appropriate, but also *how* the particular penalty was selected.

Moral: Work closely with the personnel specialists responsible for advising your organization in selecting the appropriate penalty, and document your thought process in making the final determination of penalty; such notes can be extremely helpful down the road in preparing to explain your actions at an arbitration, Merit Systems Protection Board (MSPB) or hearing before the Equal Employment Opportunity Commission (EEOC).

Special Considerations

A final word is in order regarding special disciplinary situations that you may encounter, namely, dealing with an employee whose misconduct may be rooted in drug or alcohol abuse.

Under both law and regulations applicable to civilian employees, the employer is required to view dependence on such substances as a handicapping condition. In addition, the employer is obliged to make efforts at *reasonably accommodating* employees with mentally or physically handicapping conditions—including drug or alcohol dependency.

Practically, what this means to you is that when an employee either appears to be dependent on alcohol or drugs, or in connection with a disciplinable infraction claims to be addicted, it is necessary to consider what reasonable accommodation may be appropriate in helping the employee to overcome the problem. The accommodation often consists of withholding discipline while the employee seeks assistance in overcoming his or her addiction, and cooperating in such efforts by approving leave or leave without pay to attend counseling or rehabilitation training.

Note, however, that being dependent on a controlled substance *does not* entitle an employee to continue behavior that violates rules or job requirements. If rehabilitation efforts do not succeed or the employee continues committing infractions, discipline—up to and including removal from the service—is appropriate.

In dealing with such situations, it clearly would be a good idea to seek assistance from the management-employee relations representatives in your servicing civilian personnel office.

Chapter Seven

Effective Performance Management

Chapter Seven

Introduction

One of your most important duties as a supervisor of Federal employees is managing employee performance.

Why Performance Ratings Are Important

Performance appraisal ratings are very important to the career of a Federal civil servant. They are used in a variety of critically important ways. For example, performance ratings are used in deciding who keeps or loses a job during a reduction-in-force (RIF). A performance rating is also a factor in making promotion selections, and in determining who will receive a performance award. A performance rating provides a basis for taking adverse action because of poor performance, which can mean a reduction in grade or even removal from the federal service. In short, the performance rating that you give to an employee has a major impact on that employee's career. Consequently, establishing performance requirements, and appraising employee performance is a job that must be taken seriously. Meeting your responsibilities will require careful planning on your part long before wading into the process of filling out appraisal forms.

For more information, see *Performance Standards Made Simple!* (Third Edition), FPMI Communications, Inc. (1991) Huntsville, AL

Overview of the Manager's Role in Performance Management

Obviously you will want to rate employees fairly. To do so you need to follow several steps. Using this organized approach will help you to make sure that employees perceive your performance management efforts as fair and objective. You will find it helpful to follow these steps:

☞ Encourage your employees to participate in the performance appraisal process by assisting in identifying primary job functions, responsibilities and objectives.

☞ Identify specific job elements; *i.e.*, key individual functions of a job— such as entering stock numbers accurately into an inventory control program.

☞ Determine which job elements are *critical*; that is, functions so important that failing to complete them correctly provides a basis for downgrading or removing an employee.

☞ Develop overall performance standards for each job which incorporate the identified elements and spell out your expected levels of quantity, quality and timeliness.

☞ Communicate performance standards and job elements to each employee clearly to establish a mutual understanding of performance expectations.

☞ Monitor each employee's performance during the year; do not wait until year's end to attempt a "snapshot" view.

☞ Evaluate each employee by comparing performance relative to each identified element in the performance standards you established earlier.

☞ Take appropriate action based on performance, such as recommending rewards for superior performance or initiating performance improvement measures for sub-standard performance.

Each of these steps is discussed briefly below to give you an idea of how to approach the performance appraisal system.

Encourage Employees to Participate

This can be done informally when you meet with the employee to begin developing a performance plan. It does not require you or the employee to put anything into writing. The purpose of employee participation is to develop a sense of "ownership" so that the employee does not feel that you have arbitrarily set job requirements. Just as important, it gives you an opportunity to discuss with the employee what she believes is important about the job, problems with the job, and opportunities to improve efficiency and productivity by eliminating unnecessary roadblocks for the employee to succeed. In most cases you will have a performance plan from the previous year that may prove helpful in writing a new one. If the job has changed, or if the old plan does not suit your requirements, do not hesitate to make necessary changes.

Setting Performance Elements and Standards

The Federal service performance appraisal process rests on the use of performance standards. In plain English, performance standards set forth the particular performance requirements or expectations that management sets for each position. Generally such standards reflect the most significant functions and objectives that an employee is expected to accomplish during a year on the job.

Well thought-out, properly developed standards and elements will help you to make objective judgments in rewarding, promoting, and retaining your best employees. Poorly written standards and elements may result in rewarding or retaining employees who may not be the most productive ones in your organization, and may result in reversing your efforts to demote or remove underachievers. The best way to develop effective standards is through a step-by-step development process that starts with identifying individual *job elements*.

Identify Job Elements

The job elements of a position may be defined as:

> *A distinguishable unit or body of work required by an employee's position and directed toward a specific goal.*

When you are identifying job elements, ask yourself these two questions:

> **What are the major functions of this job?**
>
> **Which ones are most significant, time consuming, or critical to successful accomplishments of the key duties of this position?**

Once identified, you should write down the individual job elements. One common way to write them is by listing a verb and an object. For example, in stating one job element for a secretary, you might write:

Types (verb) *letters and disposition forms* (object). Next, you should state the purpose of the element. Using the same example, you could write:

> Types letters and disposition forms *in order to* prepare documents for the Administrator.

Identifying Critical Elements

Once you have decided on the job elements, you should next decide which elements should be considered to be *critical job elements*. What is a critical job element? Here's a working definition:

> *A job element that is so important that unacceptable performance by an employee of one critical element constitutes overall unacceptable performance by the employee.*

In other words, if a civilian employee who works for you fails to meet a critical element, the failure is so significant to the job that you, as the supervisor, would have to do something about it. The "something" that you do could be anything from downgrading the employee to removing the person from Federal service—depending upon the extent of the problem.

There is no limit on the number of critical elements that may be included in a performance plan. But there must be at least one critical element in every employee's performance plan. In practice, most plans contain from three to eight critical elements.

Developing Performance Standards

Once you have written the job elements and identified the ones that are critical, you are faced with what may be the toughest part of the job: writing the performance standard. A performance standard is:

The stated level of achievement, including quality, quantity, manner of working and timeliness, for the duties and responsibilities of a position within a specific period of time.

In short, a performance plan consists of two items: first, clearly stated duties that the employee is expected to perform (*job element*); and second, an equally clear statement of how well and how quickly the employee is expected to obtain the described results (*performance standard*).

A performance standard typically measures quantity, quality or timeliness. The term *quantity* refers to the amount of work produced or a product that is produced. It can be stated in a number of different ways such as a number of items to result from the employee's work or a specific percentage of errors that will be allowed for each unit of work.

Quality refers to how well the work is performed or how accurate or complete the final product is expected to be. Quality may be expressed as accuracy, appearance, effectiveness, or some combination of these when developing a performance standard.

Timeliness refers to how quickly a product is to be produced by the employee, or the allowable time for completing various tasks.

Communicate Performance Standards and Job Elements

As we told you earlier in this chapter, you should encourage employee participation throughout the entire process of writing a performance plan. So take time to explain the plan you have written and make sure the employee understands it. *Remember also that you can change the plan at any time throughout the rating period and, in fact, you should change it as circumstances dictate.*

Monitor Performance

This should be an on-going process. As a supervisor of civilians, you are entitled to work with them at any time to help them and your organization to improve.

The first time an employee will formally receive feedback from the supervisor on his or her progress under the performance appraisal plan will be during a *progress review.* A progress review is:

> *A scheduled meeting between a supervisor and an employee to discuss the employee's progress in meeting job elements and performance standards.*

You must have at least one formal progress review during the appraisal period. Some agency plans require progress reviews at regular intervals. Even though a progress review is planned during the appraisal period, you do not have to wait until a regularly scheduled formal review to meet with your employees to discuss work performance. If daily communication is good, neither the year-end rating nor your comments will be a surprise to the employee. Progress reviews will usually benefit both you and your employees.

During a progress review, you will have an opportunity to determine whether the employee needs advice or other assistance in meeting the requirements of the performance plan. By arranging such a meeting, you will have a chance to encourage the employee to express any problems encountered during the appraisal period and to ask for any assistance necessary. Sometimes specific remedial actions may be identified, such as additional training in how to carry out a particular task.

The progress review is also a time for the supervisor to provide feedback to the employee on his or her performance during the appraisal period. Remember: The purpose of the appraisal system is not to surprise the employee at the end of the appraisal cycle but to help him (and your organization) meet its performance goals throughout the year. If you have a problem with an employee's performance, the employee should be made aware of it and reminded of your expectations. This is also a good time to acknowledge an employee's performance accomplishments. This feedback meeting will also let you know how the employee is progressing and whether any changes need to be made in the plan.

Evaluate The Employee

The final performance appraisal discussion lets the employee know where she stands. At the end of the performance cycle, you will rate the employee's performance for the entire appraisal cycle. The appraisal that you issue becomes a formal record that is maintained by the supervisor and the personnel office. As you know, it will be used in making decisions on a variety of personnel actions.

Your formal rating should not be given to the employee until the rating has been approved by your organization. The rating you issue must be reviewed—normally by the next level in the chain of command—so you do not want to create a problem for you and the rest of your management team until the final "go-ahead" has been given. This doesn't mean that you are restricted from discussing performance with any of your employees on a regular basis. It only restricts you from giving a final performance rating before final approval is received.

When you meet with any of your employees to give a performance rating, explain your reasons for the rating by going through each job element listed and indicate what the employee did that led to the rating. Unfortunately, some people (both supervisors and employees) view the rating process as a negative situation. But while the rating process may be the time at which you are identifying performance problems, it can also be a good time to highlight the positive side of an employee's performance as well. Take the time to praise good performance when it is justified. Just as you should take time to point out shortcomings. Praise, when justified, encourages a person to continue accomplishing the performance objectives of the job.

If there are negative aspects of the employee's performance, you must discuss this as well as the positive aspects even if it is unpleasant to do so. Failing to discuss negative concerns is unfair to the employee, the organization, and ultimately to the public. Remember that the employee must have an opportunity to improve. If there is a performance problem, the employee should not be denied your opinion even if you or the employee feel uncomfortable discussing it. Failing to point out such problems usually ensures they will continue. It also denies your agency the benefit of the improved performance you should be encouraging and requiring.

Take Appropriate Action

Performance appraisal can affect employees in a number of other ways—both positive and negative. As a supervisor, you are responsible for taking appropriate action based on the employee's rating. What is "appropriate action"? Any one of the following qualify, depending on the circumstances and rating received:

☞ Quality Step Increase

☞ Within-Grade Increase

☞ Performance Award

☞ Promotion

☞ Training

☞ Reassignment

☞ Demotion or Removal

In taking any of these actions, of course, you should consult with your personnel office as soon as possible after the performance rating has been issued to ensure that any recommended action is carried out promptly.

Chapter Eight

Developing Employees

Chapter Eight

Introduction

An important part of every manager's job is that of continuing the development of the people who work under your direction to ensure a productive workforce and the on-going ability to meet changing job requirements. As a Federal manager, you have several responsibilities in this area:

☞ Analyzing organizational needs and identifying specific training requirements

☞ Developing training plans for the overall organization and individual employees within it

☞ Obtaining and allocating resources effectively to accomplish training needs and produce desired gains in organizational efficiency

☞ Evaluating the impact of training efforts and making necessary adjustments to insure maximum results

What Training Can And Cannot Do

Training can develop basic skills, improve existing skills and help employees to keep pace with the shifting demands of the job caused by changes in mission, work methods, technology and organizational structure. If an employee does not know what to do or how to perform a job properly, training can be very effective. So if the purpose of training is to develop new skills, improve existing skills or to modify skills to adjust to job changes, training is probably the answer.

But there are some goals that training cannot accomplish. Training cannot alter employees basic abilities, and only rarely can it alter their attitudes toward work. Nor can it easily overcome fundamental gaps in education without extensive effort and expense. For example, if an employee lacks basic mathematical skills, training is unlikely to turn him or her into an effective Budget Analyst without an enormous investment in time and money—and maybe not even then.

Performance Based Training

The starting point of any training effort is coming to grips with the job to be done. Knowing what a job requires and how well you want it done will give you data to make training decisions. After you have a handle on the job, look at the person in it and how their skills compare to your requirements. Your Personnel or Human Resources Office has employee development specialists who can help you analyze positions and assess the individual training needs of your workers.

How To Start

Start by looking at the jobs in your organization. Use this approach to identify job requirements.

1. Using the position description, identify the major duties and responsibilities of the jobs in your unit.

2. Look at the performance standards and performance ratings of employees in the unit. Do they square with your requirements? If the standards reflect an under-use of the employees, and/or the performance ratings reflect suboptimal output, training may be indicated.

3. If either the position description or the standards are not what you want, adjust them so they accurately reflect the duties and performance levels for the position.

4. Determine whether the requirements of jobs in your organization have changed or are about to change. For example, if computers will be introduced into a functional area that has not used them up to now, it will be important to determine the type and level of training that will be necessary to bring employees up to speed.

Building in Quality

The job requirements and standards you set this month or this year should reflect current mission requirements and expected performance levels. But this should not represent a fixed, permanent expectation of individual or organizational performance levels. Your efforts to identify ways in which to continuously improve organizational performance should lead to an on-going effort to find and provide training that will continuously boost performance. In short, training dollars should be viewed as an investment that produces a measurable return in terms of improved quantity, quality and timeliness of work accomplished within the unit.

Assessing Individual Employees

The next step is deciding how each worker stands in comparison to your expectations. Trainees or entry level employees are assessed differently from those operating at the full performance level.

For new employees and those who are still climbing a career ladder to the full performance level of an occupation, most training should be geared to providing them the basic information and skills needed to progress on the job. For employees who have attained the full performance level, training should be geared to maintaining their level of expertise through exposure to new information and emerging changes in how their work is performed.

With all employees, of course, assessment of the person's performance relative to established performance standards should serve as an effective guide to areas in which additional training, coaching or counseling may be necessary.

Individual Development Plans

Once you have decided what a job is, how it works and how well you want it done at each grade level, the next step is tailoring a plan for the development of each worker, regardless of whether he or she is a new trainee or at the intermediate or full performance level.

A good individual development plan includes:

1. A list of the specific tasks and expectations of performance required of the person at their current level.

2. How the skills needed to carry them out will be acquired or improved; for example, through on-the-job training, classroom instruction, or self-study.

3. When the training will start, and who will be responsible for conducting and evaluating it.

4. What performance level must be obtained at the end of each training experience.

5. Where the person can go for additional help if needed.

Getting The Training You Need

Time and money for training are always limited. Once you have your organizational need for training, you must set priorities on the use of your resources.
Here are several factors to consider:

1. Impact

— What would be the effect of failing to meet the training need both in the short and long run?

— What benefit would come to the overall organization from the training?

— Would training one employee have a spin-off effect on other workers?

— Must the training be done to meet a mission requirement?

— Does the need for the training affect the development or productivity of an employee?

2. Scope

— How common or widespread is the need?

— Where in the organization does it show up?

— How many people are affected?

3. Out Of Your Control

— Is the training mandated?

— Has top management set specific priorities?

— Are there agency or installation policies that will affect your decision?

4. Time

— How soon is the training needed?

— Is there a timeframe within which the training must occur to have value?

5. Practicality

— What is the effect of the cost of the training on overall resources?

— Are there times when the training would adversely affect operations; for example, during busy seasons?

Training Sources

Training is available from a broad array of sources. Included among them are:

☞ Agency-sponsored courses

☞ Courses offered by vendors, such as FPMI

☞ OPM-sponsored training

☞ Courses at local colleges and universities

☞ Seminars by professional associations.

Training Follow Up

Once training is completed, it is critically important to assess the effect it has had on the organizations and/or the employee's performance. You may want to set up a meeting with employees immediately after formal training to "debrief" them. Similarly, you might require a written summary report of what was accomplished or learned, and how it will be applied on the job. Often the lessons learned can be passed to other employees in a summary form, thus extending the value of the training without additional cost.

Finally, periodic performance checks should be made to reinforce lessons learned in the training. If training fails to improve performance, you should look into the situation to determine whether the training itself is ineffective, or whether the individual employee requires additional assistance.

Getting Help

The professional Employee Development Specialists employed by your agency will have information on the formal training available at your installation and in local educational institutions. Most agency career management programs have established training courses for employees in each career field. Do not hesitate to ask their assistance in assessing and responding to training needs in your organization.

Chapter Nine

Agency Or Administrative Grievance Procedures

Chapter Nine

Introduction

Each agency is required to set up a grievance procedures for civilian employees who are not covered by a labor agreement with a union. (Employees who are covered by a labor agreement *must* use the negotiated grievance procedure.)

These grievance procedures give employees the opportunity to get an objective review of individual or group complaints about working conditions, employment decisions affecting them.

These procedures are usually not as broad in scope as negotiated grievance procedures. Also, some matters are excluded from coverage.

The head of the facility generally serve as the final decision authority for these grievances. Managers and supervisors are given the opportunity to resolve grievances informally before they are elevated to the head of your agency.

Grievance Rights

Employees who believe they have not been fairly treated have a right to present their grievances to management officials for consideration and a decision. An employee may file a grievance on her own behalf or may be accompanied and advised by a representative of his or her own choosing.

Matters Covered

Employees may generally file grievances on any matter of concern or dissatisfaction within the agency's control.

Exceptions to this usually include:

☞ Decisions that can be appealed to the Merit Systems Protection Board (MSPB) or is subject to final administrative review by the Office of Personnel Management (OPM) or the Equal Employment Opportunity Commission (EEOC).

☞ Nonselection from a properly constituted list or certificate of candidates for promotion.

☞ Warning notices

☞ Termination of a temporary promotion

☞ The content of critical or non-critical elements of an employee's performance standards.

☞ Granting or not granting a performance award, quality increase, or honorary award.

☞ Unadopted suggestions

☞ Merit Pay increases

☞ Probationary terminations

☞ Matters covered by a negotiated grievance procedure.

☞ Fraud, waste and abuse complaints appropriately filed with the agency or the agency's Inspector General.

How The Procedure Works

The employee and representative (if any) usually present the grievance to the employee's immediate supervisor orally, telling the supervisor that the matter is a grievance. There are time frames an employee must meet in filing a grievance.

When the supervisor receives the grievance, an attempt is made to resolve it. If the issues raised are outside the supervisor's authority and responsibility, he/she contacts the officials who may be able to help. If the supervisor cannot resolve the grievance within certain time frames, he/she will tell the employee and the employee's representative their right to go to the next step. At this point the employee is notified of the next step available and any time limits that apply.

If a grievance cannot be resolved through informal procedures, the employee may submit the grievance in writing. Generally, the grievance must explain the issues involved and the relief sought.

Formal, written grievances are handled in a variety of ways. For example, in some agencies, the grievance may be investigated and/or heard by a special office established for that purpose and a report issued to the person in charge of the facility. In others, the decision maker may personally hold a hearing or appoint a grievance examiner to hear the facts and recommend a resolution.

Deciding Official

Normally, the head of the activity who can grant the relief sought in the grievance is the deciding official. However, when the grievance involves another part of the agency or the matter grieved was originally decided by the head of the activity, the procedures usually permit a final decision by the next organizational level within the agency.

Deciding officials must consider the grievance and decide on it fairly. A good decision is based on the facts brought out during the grievance process, tracks the issues raised in the grievance and explains the rationale in clear terms.

Getting Help

Your personnel office provides technical advice to management and employees on how the procedure works and other personnel regulations that may be related to the grievance issues.

Tips on Grievance Handling

Virtually every Federal manager can count on dealing with at least some grievances during his or her career. Like every other aspect of personnel management, it is possible to do well or not so well in handling complaints. Here are several tips to bear in mind when dealing with employee grievances:

☞ *Don't take it personally.*

It is natural to view a grievance as an attack on you or one of your decisions. But it is better to look at the grievance objectively, with a sincere effort to determine what the grievant is unhappy about, and whether he or she has a valid point.

☞ *Listen more than you talk.*

Just what it sounds like. Your first task in grievance handling is to find out just what the grievant feels is wrong, why he/she thinks so, and what he/she would like you to do about it. It's hard to do all that if you're doing most of the talking. So generally confine yourself to asking helpful questions until you have a good handle on the situation.

☞ *Don't shoot from the lip.*

The most common mistake in grievance handling is giving an immediate response. It is *always* better to take the time to check out facts, confer with personnel experts if necessary, and think over the answer before you give it.

☞ *Keep things on a professional level.*

Do not argue with or yell at a grievant. This is just another part of the job, so handle it like the professional manager you are. Keep cool and give a sensible reply.

☞ *Use expert help.*

No one can be expected to know all the twists and turns of the laws, regulations and contract provisions that apply to Federal employees. So don't hesitate to ask the personnel or legal folks for some advice and assistance in developing a response to a grievance.

☞ *Explain your decision—preferably in plain English.*

It may well turn out that the grievant does not have a valid complaint and there is nothing to be done about the source of his or her unhappiness. Nevertheless, it is always important to explain how you reached your decision—regardless of whether the grievant is likely to agree or like it. An explanation at least shows that you took the time to arrive at a reasoned decision. Simply saying "no" is more like a slap in the face, and likely to just raise more resentment.

Chapter Ten

Safety In The Workplace

Chapter Ten

Providing a safe and healthy workplace is a moral and legal obligation of all employers, including the Federal government. As a manager you carry a large part of the responsibility for seeing to it that employees under your direction work safely. Your role includes:

☞ Regularly inspecting the workplace and employees' work habits to ensure that they are safe.

☞ Noting potential safety and health hazards and reporting them promptly.

☞ Taking steps to correct potential or actual hazards or unsafe work practices.

☞ Providing training, guidance and counseling to employees on how to recognize and avoid hazards and unsafe work practices.

☞ Reporting accidents and injuries promptly and accurately.

☞ Lead by example through careful adherence to agency safety rules.

Keeping Safety in Perspective

Working safely is essential to the, well, health of any organization. The simple fact of the matter is that accidents are costly, both to individual employees and to the agency. Accordingly, it is critical that every manager and employee in the organization take an active part in spotting and correcting hazards and unsafe work practices. Above all, remember that safety is not just the job of the agency's designated safety specialists.

Identifying Safety Risks

As a manager it is your responsibility to make sure that employees under your direction routinely follow special safety requirements for their jobs. For example, if a position or particular task requires eye, ear or foot protection, make sure that you communicate these requirements to employees and regularly check to make sure they are being followed.

In addition, it is important to pay particular attention to the following workplace features to identify and correct potential hazards:

☞ Motor vehicles and operating methods

☞ Walking surfaces

☞ Stairs

☞ Furniture and office equipment

☞ Storage areas

☞ Exits

☞ Fire hazards, such as piles of boxed paper

☞ Electrical equipment

☞ Cords, wires and other floor-level hazards

☞ Open file drawers and elevator doors

☞ Blocked exits

☞ Employees apparently impaired by drugs or alcohol

Promptly report any potential safety hazard to your agency's Personnel or Safety office and follow-up to make sure the problem is promptly fixed.

Job Safety Analysis

In an effort to head-off problems before they arise, agencies often encourage managers and employees to engage in job safety analysis. It consists of an organized approach that breaks a particular job or function into a sequence of specific steps, then identifies the potential hazards of each step, and recommends safe job procedures to be applied.

It is a good idea to apply Job Safety Analysis (JSA) to any new job that may include potential hazards, as well as to jobs that have resulted in employee injuries or complaints of hazardous conditions.

Reporting Injuries

Although every manager hopes it will never be necessary, chances are that at one point or another you may have to deal with an on-the-job injury or job-related illness.

In the event of a medical emergency, you will be required to complete one or more forms related to the injury or illness. They include the following:

☞ **Form CA-1** is used to report a traumatic injury and claim for continuation of pay or compensation.

☞ **Form CA-2** is used to report an occupational disease and claim for compensation.

☞ **Form CA-2a** is used to report the recurrence of a traumatic injury or occupational disease.

☞ **Form CA-16** is used to authorize immediate medical treatment in connection with a job-related injury.

Personnel specialists can provide you with the necessary forms and assistance in filling them out. It is critically important that you fill the correct forms out accurately and promptly, since an employee's continued compensation after an on-the-job injury or illness depends upon your doing so.

Legal Liability

Federal managers have generally not been held liable for personal injury suits filed by employees who have been injured or who contracted a disease in the workplace. Nevertheless, Federal courts appear to be changing their views somewhat, in that they have upheld the criminal prosecution of several Federal managers for criminal misconduct in allowing toxic chemicals to be improperly discharged in violation of various environmental laws.

Whether the doctrine of sovereign immunity will continue to shield Federal managers from claims of negligence leading to illness or injury remains open to speculation. Consequently, for a variety of reasons it is a good idea to be fully aware of the safety requirements of the job and to make a diligent and continuing effort to see to it that employees follow safe work practices.

Chapter Eleven

Workers' Compensation

Chapter Eleven

Introduction

As a Federal manager, you will eventually find that one or more of your employees may be entitled to benefits under the Federal Employees' Compensation Act (FECA). This law provides benefits to Federal employees injured on the job or who suffer a disabling employment-related disease or illness. Benefits provided under the FECA are the only remedy against the government for work-related injuries or death.

The program is administered by the Office of Workers' Compensation Programs (OWCP) within the Department of Labor. This is why you may frequently hear this program referred to as the "OWCP" or "worker's comp" program. Your role in administering this program, while not extensive, is very important because knowing what you should do and where to go for help may save you and your agency considerable time, frustration and money.

OWCP has responsibility for making rules and regulations governing the program. But more importantly the FECA makes them—not you—responsible for making decisions on claims filed by a Federal employee. The amount of money involved in some of these decisions may be significant. For example, some of the benefits provided by the program include medical care, disability compensation payments, vocational rehabilitation, continuation of pay because of a work-related injury, partial payment of funeral and burial expenses and compensation payments to surviving dependents.

The Supervisors' Role

In order to meet your responsibilities for the OWCP program, here are a couple of definitions you need to know:

Traumatic Injury

A traumatic injury is a wound or other harm to the body caused by external force, including stress or strain. The injury must be identifiable as to time and place of occurrence and member or function of the body affected. It must also be caused by a specific event or incident within a single day or work shift. (Example: employee hits his thumb with a hammer or employee slips and falls)

Occupational Disease / Illness

An occupational disease or illness is distinguishable from a traumatic injury in that it is produced over a longer period of time. The most common types are systemic infection; continued or repeated stress or strain; exposure to toxins, poisons or fumes, or other continued and repeated exposure to conditions of the work environment. (Example: hearing loss, carpel tunnel syndrome.)

Continuation of Pay (COP)

The FECA provides that an employee's regular pay may be continued for up to 45 calendar days. This provision is intended to eliminate interruption of the employee's income while the claim is being processed. COP includes any premium pay, night or shift differential, Sunday or holiday pay, and other extra pay, except overtime.

Controversion

An agency's decision to contest an employee's request for continuation of pay.

Compensation

If disability extends beyond 45 days, the employee is eligible to receive compensation for loss of her wages. Compensation is paid at a rate of 66 2/3% of the employee's pay without dependents and 75% with one or more dependents. Compensation continues as long as the employee is out of work due to the injury or illness.

Responsibilities

As a Federal manager or supervisor, you have several responsibilities under this program. Generally, it is your role to:

☞ Report all accidents and injuries and arrange for immediate medical treatment for injured employees.

☞ Advise employees of their rights under the Federal Employees' Compensation Act.

☞ Keep employees informed of the procedures to follow if they are injured on the job or if they should suffer a disabling employment related disease or illness. Also you should advise employees about the possible penalties for falsifying claims or reports.

☞ Keep your payroll office informed about an employee's use of "traumatic" leave so that continuation of pay may be properly charged.

☞ Provide, if available, light or limited duty that is within the employee's medical restrictions.

Use Your Personnel Office For Assistance

Obviously, you cannot be expected to know or keep up with the latest changes or technical requirements of the program. Your personnel office will be able to give you or your employees information you need about the program such as:

☞ How to obtain, complete, and submit any required forms to the Department of Labor.

☞Advice on benefits such as medical care, continuation of pay, minimum and maximum compensation, rehabilitation and its relationship to the retirement program, life insurance and placement assistance.

☞ Circumstances likely to cause loss or reduction of compensation.

☞ Assistance for dependents if an employee has died.

☞ Information to employees about procedures on hearings, reconsideration requests and appeals.

Situations That May Arise

There are several fairly common situations involving this program that may arise and which will require you to take some action. In general, you should prepare a written report of every injury or occupational disease when it is likely to:

☞ result in a medical charge against OWCP;

☞ result in disability for work beyond the day of the injury or the shift on which the injury occurred;

☞ require treatment;

☞ result in future disability;

☞ result in permanent disability; or

☞ result in continuation of pay.

The Department of Labor uses forms (called the CA-1 and CA-2 forms) you must use for this. These forms are normally available in your personnel office.

Notice of Injury, Occupational Disease or Death

If an employee sustains a traumatic injury that occurred while performing official duties, the employee should give a written notice of the injury to his supervisor using the CA-1 form. If the employee has an employment related disease or disability, this must be reported by the employee on Form CA-2. If one of your employees should die while performing official duties, OWCP should be notified by telephone.

Your personnel representative will help you handle any of these situations so it is a good idea to discuss it with this person to save yourself unnecessary frustration.

Compensation Claims

As noted above, the FECA provides benefits to employees that may result in an employee receiving compensation, medical benefits or rehabilitation training. There are a number of forms that are used in these cases and your personnel representative should be able to provide you with a copy and explain when and how each one is used.

Supervisor's Responsibility in COP Cases

After you have been notified that an employee has suffered an employment related traumatic injury that requires medical treatment, you should take the following steps:

☞ If appropriate, authorize medical care by submitting Department of Labor form CA-16 (usually available in your personnel office) to your health unit or to a qualified doctor or hospital in the area. Note: employees are guaranteed the right to choose any licensed physician.

☞ Provide the employee with Form CA-1 for reporting the injury. After you receive the completed form, return the "Receipt of Notice of Injury" back to the employee.

☞ Advise the employee of the right to elect to receive continuation of regular pay or to use annual or sick leave, if the injury is disabling.

☞ Determine if the agency is going to controvert the continuation of pay and, if so, whether the employee's pay will be terminated.

☞ Make sure that the CA-1 form (completed by both the supervisor and the employee) are sent to the Department of Labor. The law allows 30 days for the filing of a notification of injury. If you take the full thirty days, however, the employee is likely to have an interruption of income. Before sending in the form, you should discuss the matter with your servicing personnel office.

Contesting An Employee's Claim

When an agency objects to paying an employee's claim for continuation of pay, this is called "controversion." Your agency may controvert a claim by completing a portion of the CA-1 form and submitting detailed information to OWCP.

Normally, your agency will continue to pay the employee even if the claim is controverted. This does not always happen, however, and the agency will not continue the employee's pay if:

☞ The disability is a result of an occupational disease or illness (see the definitions at the beginning of the chapter);

☞ The employee is not a citizen or a resident of the United States, Canada, or the Panama Canal Zone (i.e., he is a foreign national employed outside of these areas);

☞ The injury occurred off the employing agency's premises and the employee was not engaged in official duties at the time;

☞ The employee caused the injury by willful misconduct or intended to bring about her injury or death;

☞ The employee's intoxication was the cause of the injury;

☞ The injury was not reported on a form approved by OWCP (usually the CA-1 form) within 30 days following the injury;

☞ The work stoppage occurred more than 90 days following the injury;

☞ The employee first reported the injury after his employment was terminated.

Please check with your servicing personnel office if you have any questions about whether your employee is entitled to COP.

Positive Payoffs For Good Management Of OWCP Claims

• Improved safety and lower lost-time rates,

• Raise morale and boost productive time,

• Retaining injured employees in productive assignments

• Elimination of erroneous claims

• Reduced costs

Remember, as a supervisor, your job is to see that employees get all the benefits to which they are entitled but you should also ensure that employees who are fully or partially recovered are provided useful work and are removed from the OWCP rolls.

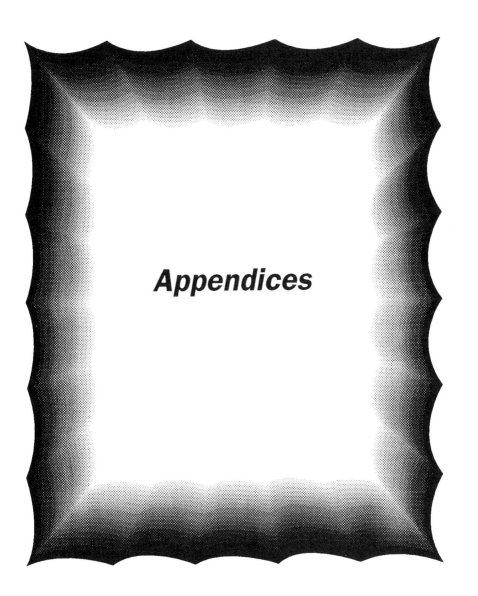

Appendices

Appendix A

Sample Position Description

TITLE: File Clerk GS-305-2

MAJOR DUTIES

Incumbent performs a combination of the following duties:

Receives and sorts documents into like categories by alphabet, date, or other similar classification. Files/re-files materials in established file folders identified by name, social security number, numerical control number or other file designation. Inserts materials into corresponding folder and ensures proper arrangement of contents such as placement on left or right side, chronological filing by date or other established procedure.

Assists users of the filing system by retrieving file (s) from bins, shelves, drawers or similar file containers. Requests may be in person or submitted in written form. Completes charge out card or other control record with date, users name/activity, etc. Obtains any required signatures for receipt of files and releases files; files charge-out card/control card in designated area for accountability.

Prepares file labels for new files. Follows examples and procedures contained in regulations or office guides for placement of information onto label and to affix label onto folder. Follows instructions to move filed materials from one designated area to another based on disposition instructions.

Prepares routine reports. Extracts available information to complete work counts, usage, or other types of reports related to files. Computes subtotals, totals or similar mathematical computations.

Receives and/or places telephone calls to verify, report, obtain or exchange information related to files. Performs routine search for record material when search is limited to a few designated or obvious places within the files or readily identified locations outside the files unit.

Performs other duties as assigned.

FACTOR 1 - KNOWLEDGE REQUIRED BY THE POSITION
Knowledge of filing procedures and operations to sequence materials, match items to be filed in the corresponding folder, locate items from specific sources and refile items in an existing system. Skill to write in a legible manner in order to prepare charge-out cards and/or other control documents.

Ability to communicate to exchange information related to files.

FACTOR 2 - SUPERVISORY CONTROLS
Assigned work is performed independently following established procedures. Supervisor is available to resolve unusual problems. Work is reviewed for accuracy and promptness by systematic spot-check.

FACTOR 3 - GUIDELINES

Both oral and written guidelines are specific and complete and most of them may be readily memorized. Employee works in conformance to guides, referring deviations to the supervisor.

FACTOR 4 - COMPLEXITY

Work involves arranging and filing materials in alphabetical or numerical order. Performs related duties to include searching for missing files where actions and steps to be taken are easily discernible.

FACTOR 5 - SCOPE AND EFFECT

The purpose of the work is to provide efficient mail service to serviced units. Performance of these functions on a timely basic facilitates the work performed in the serviced units.

FACTOR 6 - PERSONAL CONTACTS

Contacts are with employees in the immediate unit and with personnel from serviced units.

FACTOR 7 - PURPOSE OF CONTACTS

The purpose of contacts is to provide or obtain information related to the immediate work unit.

FACTOR 8 - PHYSICAL DEMANDS

The work requires prolonged periods of standing, walking, bending, stooping, reaching and pulling in filing activities.

Requires constant reading and adjustment to various shades of printed materials (very light to dark) which may cause eye strain. As required, employee is responsible for moving work related materials to and from the work area not to exceed 40 pounds.

FACTOR 9 - WORK ENVIRONMENT
The work is performed in an office, secure files area or similar setting; there is adequate heat, light and ventilation.

Appendix B

Sample Crediting Plan

Position: Clerk-typist GS-4

FACTOR: Ability to type government correspondence

Level III (40 points) Superior ability as evidenced by substantial experience typing Government correspondence with outstanding performance ratings.

Level II (25 points) average ability as demonstrated by Moderate experience in typing Government correspondence with fully successful ratings.

Level I (10 points) anything less

FACTOR: Knowledge of agency standard filing system

Level III (25 points) Superior ability as evidenced by substantial experience in agency filing system with outstanding ratings.

Level II (15 points) Average ability as demonstrated by moderate experience in agency filing system with fully successful ratings.

Level I (5 points) Anything less

FACTOR: Ability to type reports

Level III (25 points) Superior ability as demonstrated by substantial experience typing reports with outstanding ratings

Level II (15 points) Average ability as demonstrated by moderate experience typing reports with fully successful ratings

Level I (5 points) anything less

FACTOR: Awards

Level II (10 points) One or more Sustained Superior Performance awards in a clerical position

Level I (5 points) Other performance awards

Appendix C

SELECTION CRITERIA
POSITION: Clerk-typist GS-4

1. Knowledge of filing structures   25 points

   Agency specific technical knowledge   25 points
   Technical filing systems knowledge   20 points
   General Knowledge points   15 points
   Knowledge based on training only   10 points
   No filing background   0 points

2. Knowledge of administrative   25 points
   structure

   Sorting and distributing mail
   Making government travel
   arrangements including preparing
   orders and vouchers   5 points
   Ordering and accounting for supplies   5 points
   Preparing time cards   5 points
   Using a word processor   5 points

3. Ability to work with less than normal
   supervision   25 points

   From interview:
   Cites numerous instances,   25 points
   gives examples
   Cites moderate number   15 points
   of instances
   Cites one instance   5 points

4. Knowledge of technical report formats   25 points

Agency specific technical knowledge	25 points
Technical knowledge	20 points
General knowledge of reports	15 points
Knowledge from training class only	10 points
No Knowledge	0 points

Maximum score 100 points

FPMI Training Seminars for Federal Supervisors and Managers

The Federal Personnel Management Institute, Inc. specializes in training seminars for Federal managers and supervisors. These seminars can be conducted at your worksite at a per person rate that is substantially less than open enrollment seminars.

Each seminar includes a workbook with copies of all workshops and materials presented during the seminar. For a nominal charge the book appropriate for each seminar will also be included.

The instructors for FPMI seminars have all had practical experience with the Federal Government and know problems Federal supervisors face and how to deal effectively with those problems. FPMI also conducts specialized training seminars for personnel practitioners as well.

Some of the seminar-workshops available from FPMI include:

"The Federal Drug Testing Program"

"Preventing Sexual Harassment"

"Dealing With Problem Employees"

"Managing Unionized Employees Effectively"

"How to Write Effective Performance Standards"

"Basic Labor Relations Workshop"

"Negotiations Workshop"

"Managing Labor Relations Conflict"

"Managing Cultural Diversity"

For more information contact FPMI at:

**Federal Personnel Management Institute, Inc.
PO Box 16021
Huntsville, AL 35802-6021
(205) 882-3042**

Other Publications Available From FPMI Communications, Inc.

To order copies of any publications from FPMI Communications, call or send your order to:

FPMI Communications, Inc.
PO Box 16021
Huntsville, AL 35802-6021
(205) 882-3042
Fax (205) 882-1046

FPMI publications include:

The Federal Manager's Survival Guide ($8.95)

Federal Employment Law Practitioner's Handbook ($49.95)

Managing The Civilian Workforce: A Guide for the Military Manager ($8.95)

Performance Standards Made Simple!: A Practical Guide for Federal Managers and Supervisors ($8.95)

The Federal Manager's Guide to Discipline ($8.95)

Practical Ethics for the Federal Employee ($8.95)

The Federal Manger's Guide to TQM ($8.95)

Managing Leave and Attendance Problems: A Guide for the Federal Supervisor ($8.95)

The Federal Manager's Guide to EEO ($8.95)

The Supervisor's Guide to Federal Labor Relations ($8.95)

The Desktop Guide to ULP's ($35.00)

The Federal Manager's Guide to Preventing Sexual Harassment ($8.95)

Sexual Harassment and the Federal Employee ($4.95)

The Federal Supervisor's Guide to Drug Testing ($8.95)

The Federal Employee's Guide to Drug Testing ($2.95)

The Bargaining Book: A Guide to Collective Bargaining in the Federal Government ($9.95)

The Union Representative's Guide to Federal Labor Relations
($8.95)

The Federal Labor & Employee Relations Update ($195.00) (The *Update* is a monthly publication. The price is for a one year subscription.)

The Federal Manager's Edge ($45.00) (The *Edge* is a monthly newsletter specifically written for Federal managers.)

The *MSPB Alert!* is a monthly Bulletin of recent decisions of the Merit Systems Protection Board. The price is $125.00 per year or $95.00 per year if ordered in conjunction with the *Federal Labor & Employee Relations Update*.

Quantity discounts are available for all publications from FPMI Communications. For more information, please call or fax your request to us.

If you would like to order any of the books listed above, please fill in the order form below. We ask that you allow 3 weeks for delivery.

ORDER FORM

Name of Book	Quantity	Price	Total

Shipping charge for 1-10 books $3.50. For large orders please call FPMI Communications, Inc. for actual UPS charges.

We ask that all orders be **Prepaid** or be accompanied by a **Government Purchase Order**. If you would like to charge this order using your MasterCard, Visa, Diners Club or Carte Blanche call FPMI Communications today.

Video Based Training Programs
Developed Specifically For
Federal Managers and Supervisors

• *Managing Under a Labor Agreement*

• *Managing Under the Labor Relations Law*

Package includes both video programs with 25 workbooks for each course and 25 copies to *The Supervisors Guide to Federal Labor Relations*. (Complete Price $895.00)

• *Sexual Harassment: Not Government Approved*

• *Preventing Sexual Harassment: Some Practical Answers*

Package includes both video programs with 25 workbooks and a Leader's Guide, 25 copies of *The Federal Supervisors Guide to Preventing Sexual Harassment* and 25 copies of *Sexual Harassment and The Federal Employee*. (Complete Price $895.00)

To order any of our publications, training seminars, or videotapes, please call FPMI at (205) 882-3042. Fax us your order at (205) 882-1046 or send by mail to:

FPMI Communications, Inc.
PO Box 16021
Huntsville, AL 35802-6021

FPMI Communications Will

Customize Our Books For Your

Agency

FPMI Communications, Inc. will customize any of our books to meet specific needs of your agency. For example, if you would like to incorporate a specific policy or procedure unique to your agency or to include an introductory letter from the head of your agency or organization to all employees, this can often be quickly and easily incorporated.

Depending upon the extent of the changes necessary and the size of your order, this can often be done at little of no additional cost to your agency.

For more information on our book customizing program, call or write to FPMI Communications, Inc. at the address given on the title pages.